# WOUNDED HEARTS MADE WHOLE

*By Dr. Shari D. Scott*

ISBN-13: 978-1-63769-258-5

ISBN-10: 978-1-63769-259-2

Printed in the United States of America

# DEDICATION

A special "Thank You" to my mom for giving me permission to share our story. May our obedience and transparency pave the way for others to take the necessary path to obtain deliverance, redemption, and wholeness through Christ.

# ACKNOWLEDGMENTS

First of all, I would like to thank my heavenly Father, who gave me the will to complete this assignment. Without Him, I can do nothing. And to a few of His wonderful, faithful sons and daughters: my mother, Glenzetta Perry, whose desire for truth and transparency is second to none; my Auntie Renall Cannon, whose love and passion for Christ ignited a fire inside of me; Apostle Ronald C. Hill, whose ministry saved my life; Brenda Talley, Donna LaMothe, and Paula Moorefield, who opened their hearts and homes; all of my wonderful brothers and sisters who I can always call on and know they will be there for me; Andrea Wilson, Toi Lewis, and Patrick Thomas, three of my oldest and dearest faithful friends, to my church family, Greater New Light Baptist Church, pastored by my mentor and friend, Dr. Patrick D. Ross, and my village:

*Thank you for your love, encouragement, prayers, and support. I never could have finished this project without you! May God continue to bless you and reward you richly for all the labor of love you have shown to me! I love each and every one of you dearly.*

# INTRODUCTION

I cannot tell you how happy I am that my heavenly Father has allowed you to spend time in the pages you're about to read. I received a commandment from the Lord to write about the events of my life that have brought me to this level, and I must admit it caught me by surprise. My first reaction was one of shock, and that is putting it mildly. I recoiled, even shuddered at the thought of revisiting and revealing my past scars as I began to pray in earnest: "Lord, you're kidding, right?"

You see, I had finally gained a level of respectability among my peers, and I was even regarded as a highly anointed woman of God with a great ministry ahead. In my mind, writing this book would be ministry suicide; like pressing the delete button on a computer file and erasing my ministry before it really got started. So, I did what a lot of Christians would do in my shoes; *I began to rebuke these thoughts out of my mind!* You know, all the things we do to pretend we haven't really heard a word from God, especially when He reveals something we don't particularly want to do (*smile*). Yet in the midst of my justification as to why this could *never* be the will of God for my life, the words of Prophet Juanita Bynum came to my mind: "*How can you help somebody if you don't tell them where you have been?*"

That immediately silenced any arguments I had. I would love to tell you I instantly submitted to God's will for my life after this great revelation, but I was still very reluctant to share my past and reveal my scars. That was until I began to reminisce on the *years of tears*—years of suffering from low self-esteem and thinking I never measured up; all of the hurt, guilt, and pain I had endured and tried unsuccessfully to cover up; years of mental torment asking myself that infamous question, "Why me?" over and over again.

When I seriously considered all the years of fear, confusion, frustration, isolation, loneliness, rejection, and pain, I realized I had to write. My friend, if my testimony will deter even one person from years of suffering by sharing the revelations I have found in Christ, then I assure you it will have been worth it all.

### *My Prayer Request*

Father God, I thank you for the opportunity to share the experiences you have allowed me to go through. I thank you Lord Jesus that you are, and shall forever be, my Great Deliverer. I know there is nothing too hard for you. Father, I also know it is your sincere desire to see your children set free. You came to earth and eventually died on a tree so that we might experience life more abundantly. Therefore, I pray for your word to prevail in the life of this reader right now.

Father, I come against any spirits of doubt, confusion, fear, and frustration. In the name of Jesus, I command them to go! Release the mind of any reader struggling with despair and depression right now! Increase their faith and let them know you came to set the captive free. And through the word of faith they too can be healed, restored, and delivered out of emotional bondage!

Father, just as you have restored the years the enemy has stolen from me through lies, bitterness, seduction, and betrayal, may the eyes of this reader be flooded with light even now.

May they begin to perceive the magnitude of the love you have for them. I pray that your love will penetrate the very depths of their souls as you reveal the source of their hurt. Grace them to process the pain and plant seeds of truth, comfort, and hope in its place. Lord, allow the seed of your word to fall into hearts that are receptive and prepared to receive the truth. Then, allow your word to grow and blossom into a life that is full of grace and glory.

Father, I pray that you would replace the years that were filled with degradation, pity, and self-loathing with your love, mercy, and truth. May each reader realize what your Word (the Bible) truly is: an indispensably powerful weapon that has the ability to overcome any pain and replace it with peace, laughter, love and joy; a joy that is beyond description! For this and more I pray in Jesus' name, amen.

*My Savior and My Lord!*

# TABLE OF CONTENTS

# PROLOGUE

One Saturday morning, memories of my past came flooding to the forefront of my mind. I had just enjoyed a wonderful season of prayer. For the last few months, my Friday nights had been devoted to the Lord. I would often turn off my phone to read, pray, and study the word of God. The previous night had been awesome, and I was at peace with God and the world. Rising to make my bed, I suddenly heard the cries of a very young child coming out of nowhere. She sounded so young—maybe around three or four years old.

At first, I did not realize where the cries were coming from. There were no small children living on my floor, and no children playing outside, yet the cries continued to grow louder and louder as did my curiosity. I began to wonder why no one was going to check on the child. *"Where are her parents and why are they letting her cry for so long? Why are they ignoring her?"*

The longer she cried, the more agitated I became. For some inexplicable reason, it was as if I could feel her pain, and all of a sudden it was just too much for me to take. Falling to my knees, I began to cry uncontrollably for this little child—and that's when it hit me; somewhere deep down inside, I was the little child crying!

Not fully understanding what was happening to me, I began to do some serious praying!

*"Lord, what's going on?"*

The reply came quickly as the following words fell into my spirit. Reaching for a pen, I began to write…

*Don't leave, Daddy.*
*Please don't leave me*
*Here all alone!*

*Daddy, if you leave*
*Who's gonna protect me*
*From all the bad men*
*Waiting to pounce all over me?*

*Daddy, what you don't see*
*Is my future covered with bloodied hands*
*That have invaded my privacy.*

*Years will pass before it will come to light,*
*Yet I will always be left to wonder*
*If it could have been avoided*
*If only you had stayed in sight.*

*Oh Daddy, please don't go!*
*Even though you cannot see*
*In my heart, Daddy,*
*You mean the world to me!*

As the tears began to subside, I looked over the words wondering what caused this surge of emotions. I had no idea what I was supposed to do with this poem, but the Holy Spirit did and like a good travel guide, He began to point out the next stage of my journey.

In a very gentle voice I heard the Holy Spirit say,

*"Write your testimony."*

Write my testimony? *Write my testimony?* Casting the poem aside, I got up. I was thirty-eight years old, and unlike the make-believe fairy tale where the valiant hero comes to rescue the beautiful heroine, my life's reflection was more like a roller coaster that seemed to plummet downward at a breakneck speed.

In all fairness, there had been quite a few peaks, but like the nature of a rollercoaster, I found myself spiraling too fast around an unexpected bend and experiencing the nauseating sensation that comes from hitting a sudden drop.

I had done a great job of hiding most of my insecurities, fears, and indiscretions—or so I thought. Now, here I was on the cutting edge of ministry and exposing such secrets as mine would certainly be suicide—at least in my mind. Hence, the idea of writing my secrets seemed almost laughable. *Why on earth would I ever want to do that?*

At the time, I did not understand that I had some "daddy issues" that had never been resolved. I did not understand that God wanted to take me on a journey that would uncover and explain so much of the emotional distortion and disaster that had tainted my life for years. Before I decided to ignore His guidance completely, I decided to pray one more time.

*"Father, even if I were to write my testimony I wouldn't know where to begin?"*

The response came in a very soft and gentle voice:

*"The beginning. Start at the beginning."*

## THE BEGINNING

Some might say I had the best of both worlds. I was born in a two-parent home and my parents loved all four of their children dearly. On the surface, my parents were well off. My dad was a civil engineer who, after completing his time in the military, had graduated in the top 10 percent of his college class.

College—that is where he met my mom; a beautiful coed who captivated his attention from the first time he saw her. My dad, who worked in the cafeteria, made it a point to ask her out every time she came in. One day he got lucky as she agreed to go out with him on one condition: he would give her a free lunch. Little did he know, she was just responding to a bet she had made with her girlfriends.

Mom agreed to marry Daddy after college. Already a homeowner, he soon purchased another house to take care of his growing family. My mom always said Daddy was a good provider, and had a wonderful way with his children. Daddy loved having his children around. He even worked two jobs so his wife could stay at home. So what went wrong?

According to my mom, their problems started shortly after I was born. Mom said she wanted to go out with her friends. Daddy had encouraged her to go, and even promised to stay home and watch the children. When she returned at the appointed time, she met a drunken husband who was sick with jealousy. He said the mere thought of her being out there without him drove him crazy, and he slapped her so hard she went stumbling into the other room. Terrified, she ran into their bedroom and locked the door, only coming out after he was gone.

After two weeks, and many gifts, she agreed to stay if he promised to never hit her again and attend counseling. Things got better for a while, but inevitably the drinking and jealous rages started again. Weary of Daddy's explosive temper and jealous rages, my mom decided it was time for us to move back to her parents' home and file for a divorce. I was three or four years old—too young to understand the dynamics of what occurred between my parents. All I remember is the excitement I had whenever Daddy came by. I loved my daddy, and I didn't understand why he wasn't coming home.

I will never forget the day Daddy brought his new wife and their brand-new baby for us to meet. I don't remember much after that visit except the fact that we saw very little of Daddy afterwards.

"Even if my father and mother should desert me,
You will take care of me" (Ps. 27:10 CEV).

## STOLEN INNOCENCE

They Say Every Girl's
First Love Is Her Father
Well If This Is True
Will Someone Please Tell Me
What's A Girl Supposed To Do
When Daddy Is No Longer
There for You?

Mom began to be detached. As far back as she could remember, she had placed other people's needs before her own: her demanding mother, an over-zealous father, a jealous husband, her children, even God. Now she was ready to have some fun. She was still young, very beautiful, and discovered she loved to dance. It was during this season that she met some new friends. One in particular had a son who took a fancy to me.

### Molestation
"The act of subjecting someone to unwanted or improper sexual advances or activity."

My mom always said I was a show-me child: the type of child who wouldn't believe what you said unless it was shown. It was that natural inclination that caused the big secret waiting in the garage to be so captivating. My mother had a close male friend whom she considered a brother whose son was several years older than I was. One day, he enticed me to come to the garage to see a big secret that was hidden. Curiosity got the best of my young mind, and even though I was afraid of the dogs that stayed there, I went. I soon entered and began poking around looking for the big secret.

"So, where is the big surprise? I don't see anything out here."

"It's in the car. You have to lie down in the back seat to find it."

Complying with his instructions, I climbed into the back seat as I was told to and began to lie down when suddenly, I could feel him climbing on top of me. I began to protest.

"DJ, get off of me! You are hurting me!"

In a less than friendly voice he replied, "If you don't lie down and be still, I will let the dogs get you!"

I was terrified of dogs, and now terrified of DJ. In order to get me to come to the garage, DJ had carried me on his shoulders promising me he would not let the dogs get me. At the time, I felt safe and protected, but now I knew the true meaning of fear. I didn't want him to let the dogs get me, but I didn't want him on top of me either. There was no way of escape. My mind went blank, and the last thing I remember him doing was unzipping his pants and telling me I had better not tell.

Someone once told me you know when a wound is healed if you touch it and it doesn't hurt. Looking back, I don't know what hurts more—the fact that someone took advantage of my innocence to gratify their own selfish desire, or the fact that I didn't feel like I had anyone I could tell. How is it possible that a little girl can go into a garage with an older boy, get molested, and come out and say nothing to anyone? The answer is simple—fear. I was terrified. Where was my protection? Why didn't they recognize the change in my behavior? Were they too involved in their world to see the changes going on in mine? It would be many years before I would discover these answers.

## DADDY COME BACK

Life changed dramatically when my dad moved away. Money was scarce, and we had numerous chores. But my mom had a lot of pride, and she was determined to take care of us even though times were lean. Back then, money and food were meager. Often we wore each other's hand-me-downs as school clothes. Christmas usually consisted of a new outfit to wear to church and one or two toys. We discovered the meaning of food stamps, and how to pick our tennis shoes out of a bin at the local grocery store.

Even though times were hard, my mom taught us to be proud. She instilled a certain amount of pride in all of us. She used to always say, *"Reach for the moon and if you miss there is nothing wrong with falling among the stars."*

We knew not to bring home bad grades, and not to cause her any embarrassment. She believed in running a strict household and had her hands full trying to separate us from killing each other as fights ran rampant in our household. We were a family with issues. But despite that, we learned how to stick together and never allowed anyone from the outside to pick on us.

My mom loved her children and tried hard to make life fun again. One summer, she announced that she had a special treat for us. We were going to summer camp. It was to be held at the Baptist church right down the street from our elementary school. I was nine years old, and this would be my first time attending a summer camp.

For a while, everything was great. A van picked us up in the morning and dropped us off in the evening. We spent the whole day playing, swimming, eating snacks, and sleeping.

One day, I was selected to be a personal assistant to one of the youth counselors. My job was to help watch the younger children, help prepare the snacks, and get the supplies. With the extra duties came extra snacks and the privilege of hanging out with the older workers while the younger children slept. When the younger children would lie down for their nap, my counselor would take me upstairs to get more supplies.

One day during this period, my counselor took me upstairs to help bring down extra supplies. Once upstairs he placed me on his lap and began to touch me all over telling me how special I was. This became a regular occurrence.

At first, I enjoyed the special attention. He told me not to tell anyone, saying that it was our "little secret." But after a while, I started growing uncomfortable. Something just didn't seem right. My daddy never touched me this way.

Finally, I told him I did not want to go upstairs with him anymore. He said that meant I couldn't be his special assistant and I would no longer get special treats. I said, "I don't care," and walked out. But not before he started saying mean things to me. I started to cry, but I kept walking.

That night, I told my mother I didn't want to go back to summer camp anymore. She said I didn't have to go back if I didn't want to, and I didn't. I never told her why. I think one of the reasons was because I felt like my mom needed me, and I didn't want to add to her load. That is, my mom would tell me often how much she really admired my strength and would confide in me when she needed someone to talk to. I felt like she needed me to be strong for her and help as much as I could. Daddy didn't come around often, and Mom was always tired from working hard. I didn't want to be a burden and often kept things from her. I was a true codependent in the making if ever there was one.

# THE GOOD OLE DAYS

After my summer camp fiasco, I spent the rest of the summer playing with the children on my street. Most of the children on my block and in the surrounding neighborhood attended the same school as I did. We usually played kickball, baseball, hopscotch, colored eggs, Mother May I, jacks, pick-up sticks, double-dutch, spades, and any other games we could come up with. This was obviously before the day of electronic games.

We even made up games like seeing who could hit the ball over the electrical wires. We raced down the street to see who could roller skate the fastest. We created starting and finishing lines, and then competed with one another to see who could run, or ride their bikes, the fastest. Afterward, we would waste our money on pickles, peppermint sticks, chili Fritos, and double-scooped ice cream cones from the ice cream truck. Now those were the good ole days!

My grandparents helped to provide a stable environment for us. Shortly after the divorce was final, we moved to a new home right across the street from my grandparents. Both of them were teachers and made sure we completed our studies and stayed in line while Mom was at work.

My grandfather was also a preacher. In our house, it was mandatory that we attended church every week. Every Sunday we woke up to the smell of bacon and the sounds of a live service being played on the radio. It was my mother's custom to rise early every Sunday morning to make pancakes for all of us. We were allowed to have as many as we wanted. Then we piled into my grandfather's car and rode to church.

My grandfather believed in teaching his children and grandchildren how to work in the church at an early age. All of us learned to sing, testify, pray, and give speeches. You never knew when Granddaddy might call on you.

One day, Granddaddy got sick and started having terrible seizures. Granny said it was the wrath of God on his life. She said God had told him to return home to his kinfolk in Louisiana and help them out but Granddaddy had refused. Like Jonah, he decided he didn't want to go. That's when those terrible seizures started. Finally, he submitted to the will of God and the seizures ceased immediately.

Keeping his word, my granddaddy moved with my grandmother back to Louisiana, but not before my grandfather loaned my mother's talent to the new preacher who was renting out the little church next to Granddaddy's big church. They needed a piano player, and Granddaddy said they could borrow Mom. If only he could have known of the pastor's desires for little girls, I'm sure he would never have volunteered my mom's assistance.

## CAPTIVITY

*Little girl, little girl I've been watching you*
*Little girl, little girl I'm about to wreak havoc in your world.*
*I will use the spirit of disgrace, self-pity, and low self-esteem*
*To hinder you from walking in your true destiny.*
*And just when you think you are able to break free*
*Cords of isolation, rejection, loneliness, and fear*
*Will keep you in bondage for many more years.*

*Little girl, little girl by the time I get through*
*You will be left feeling vulnerable, frightened, abandoned, and abused.*
*And given that your hedge of protection has walked away*
*Who's going to stop me from having my way?*

Complying with my granddaddy's request, Mom went to play for the new church and took us along with her. Once again, my siblings and I helped to make up the choir and participated on a regular basis in the service. This church, however, was different in more ways than one. For one thing, this new church had the Holy Ghost. Unlike my Baptist training where we were taught to listen and be respectful in the house of God, these people were running, jumping, dancing, and rolling all over the floor! I decided I wanted to be like them. That meant I needed to be filled with the Holy Ghost also. I must admit my motives weren't exactly pure. At the time, I couldn't dance very well and I thought if I got the Holy Ghost, I would be able to dance like them.

When the preacher called for the prayer line, I decided to get in it. Back then, after the preacher finished preaching, they would have all those who wanted special prayer to stand in a prayer line. I got up with all of the others and watched as the preacher prayed for each one. I decided I would ask him to pray for me that I might receive the gift of the Holy Ghost. Kind of like Simon in the Bible except he wanted the Holy Ghost for profit; I just wanted Him so I could dance.

I was scared and excited at the same time. I had never done anything like this and didn't know quite what to expect. However, visions of a lightning bolt striking my spirit and knocking me to ground only to get up shouting probably wouldn't be too far off the mark. With the music still playing, and the saints praying, the preacher asked me a question.

*"Aren't you the little sister who gave her first testimony tonight?"*

*"Yes I am!"*

*"How old are you?"*

*"Eleven"*

*"You did a good job! Keep on testifying, okay?"*

*"Okay!"*

I felt special. I have always loved attention, and receiving it from the man of God was exhilarating. I was sure I would be shouting and dancing in a few minutes, too. Continuing to smile, he looked down at me and asked:

*"What is it that you want the Lord to do for you?"*

Very bravely, I stepped up to the plate and stated my request:

*"I want to be filled with the Holy Ghost."*

To me, it seemed as if he was surprised by my request, but he prayed for me nonetheless. My faith was high—maybe too high. Until that night, I had not seen anything so unconventional in a church before. Perhaps my disappointment wouldn't have been so great if I hadn't already planned how it was supposed to happen. It would be a number of years before someone would explain to me that the Holy Ghost is not jumping, shouting, singing or dancing only. It is the power to become a witness!

It's seems strange now, but back then, when things didn't turn out the way I thought, for some reason I remember thinking that maybe God didn't like me. My rationale was based on what I saw. To me it seemed as if everybody who received prayer got just what he or she wanted, but I didn't *feel* anything. As those thoughts came to my mind, the preacher began to petition God: "*God, please make an exception for her.*"

That was all I needed to hear. *In my mind it was settled; I wasn't good enough to receive the gift of the Holy Ghost!* Shaken, I headed back to my seat as an unworthy person. Somewhere between the altar and the empty walk back to my seat, I received a lie into my soul. Not only was I found to be unworthy to receive the precious Holy Spirit, but I also didn't qualify to receive the Heavenly Father's attention or love. Why else wouldn't he fill me too?

Sometimes I don't think we give the spirit world enough credit. I'm not saying that demons and devils can read your mind, but I'm telling you they must have some power. I was being set up for failure and I didn't even know it!

Before I left, the preacher must have noticed my despondency because he told me to call him the next day at 11:00 a.m. I cannot tell you what that did for my spirit. My heart was racing. A man of God wanted *me* to call him. I was honored. In my mind, this was not just any man; this was a man of God!

I could hardly wait for the next day to come. It was summertime and usually I would have been outside playing with my other brother and sisters, but not today. I didn't want to be late, so I sat by the clock to make sure I called on time. When eleven o'clock came, I picked up the phone and dialed. I was so excited, that after he finished his greetings, I went straight to the point.

*"Hello, Reverend, this is Shari. You asked me to give you a call?"*

He sounded surprised and yet pleased at the same time.

*"Why, yes I did. I did ask you to give me a call."*

Smiling inwardly, I was pleased I had follow through. I loved compliments. I always have. Yet this was something more. I was extremely needy—something he immediately noticed.

*Mothers and Fathers, may I please remind you how important it is to tell your children how much you love them, and to make them feel secure in your love. If you don't, they will go outside the four walls of your home looking for love. Unfortunately our predator's (commonly known as Satan, the devil) job is to kill, steal, and destroy. He does not care who he uses or how he gets in. His number one priority is to destroy your life, and unless he is uncovered, exposed, and rebuked, that's exactly what he will do.*

The conversation continued:

*"So, are you still seeking the Holy Ghost?"*

*"Yes. I want to sing, shout and dance like I saw everyone else do."*

*"Well, the first thing you must do is to clean up your life. Make sure you are not doing anything that would offend him. Okay?"*

*"Okay!"*

I wasn't exactly sure what that meant, but I decided right then I was going to watch what I said and did...*at least until Sunday.*

Sunday finally came. I had spent the last few days trying to be good. I remembered what the preacher said and couldn't wait to see what would happen now that my life was cleaned up.

After the message, he called for all those seeking the Holy Ghost to come up front. He said something about the waters being troubled and a few stood up. There were three or four of us tarrying. I remembered watching two of my peers get up, but for some reason, I hesitated. I started thinking that if I get the Holy Ghost, I'm going to have to live like this all the time, and I wasn't sure if I could. One of the mothers nudged me to go forward, and eventually I did, but once again, I didn't get it. I figured the reason I didn't get filled was because I had looked back (like Lot's wife in the Bible). I just wasn't ready to let go of the world yet.

As I watched the others fall out under the power of the Holy Spirit and speak in new tongues I returned to my seat without being filled once again. The critical voice within me shifted into high gear as I went through the usual torture routine:

*"Why can't you do anything right? Why did you have to look back? Why couldn't you just go up front with the others? Why do you always have to doubt and mess things up? Now you will never receive the Holy Ghost!"*

As church was dismissing, the pastor requested to see me in his office. As I went to see what he wanted, I can remember thinking that I was in big trouble now. After he took all that time to help me prepare my heart to receive the Holy Ghost, I am the only one who didn't receive. Nervously, I knocked on his door.

*"You requested to see me?"*

*"Yes, I noticed you did not receive the Holy Ghost, and I wanted to pray with you personally."*

*Oh boy!* I thought. *This is my big chance!*

*"Whatever you do, don't blow it this time."*

With my hands lifted up, and my heart set on heaven, I closed my eyes, determined to receive the Holy Ghost this time. As the preacher laid hands on me, he instructed me to pray. I began to say *"Thank you, Jesus"* just as I heard the other church members do. *"Lord, fill her with the Holy Ghost."* He said.

As he held the bottle of anointing oil over me, he began to anoint my hands, my forehead, my eyes, my nose, my cheeks, my mouth, and my neck. I kept my eyes closed and hands raised as I kept saying "Thank you, Jesus" just like I had seen others do. I was excited. I was finally going to get the Holy Ghost. *Thank you Jesus!*

Then he began to unbutton my blouse and placing his hand inside my bra he began to anoint my breasts. My eyes flew open in horror, but he told me to keep praying and thanking God for the Holy Ghost. I didn't understand what was going on, but he didn't seem to act like this was anything unusual, so I kept praying. As he placed the anointing oil over each breast, he continued to pray:

*"God fill her with the Holy Ghost."*

Allowing the oil to run down my belly, he then proceeded to lift my dress. I was so afraid, but I kept my eyes shut and kept praying. After he finished anointing my body, he told me to make an appointment so he could explore with me the reason why I wasn't receiving the Holy Ghost.

My mother had sent my next-door neighbor to pick us up from church. Everyone was already in the car. When she saw me, she said I looked like I had been crying and asked me if everything was okay. I remember telling her yes. Then proceeded to explain that I was trying to get the Holy Ghost and rode home in silence.

## A CRY FOR HELP

*I was eleven years old when I began to "counsel" with my pastor. My mother said it was okay as long as I didn't share any of her personal business with him. Funny, my Mom had told me not to share what was going on in the family, and the preacher asked me not to share what happened in his office. The only person I was allowed to share with was God, and I did that inwardly, afraid I might get in trouble if someone heard what I had to say.*

I made my first appointment to meet my pastor as instructed. Mom dropped me off with a reminder not to share any of her personal business, and I walked in. He looked very regal in his high back chair. I was instructed to take a seat on the other side of the desk and he began to ask me questions about my life. Slowly I began to open up and share. I felt compassion from him. I remember thinking, "*Wow, he really cares.*"

Opening up even more, I began to openly share my thoughts about how much I missed my dad and how I didn't fit in at school. I even told him about the youth counselor at the summer camp who used to sit me on his lap and molested me. As I spoke, I remember him getting up from his big desk and pulling up a chair directly in front of me. He continued to listen intently as he placed one of his hands on my knees and massaging the top of my leg, he encouraged me to keep talking.

I remember thinking how nice his hand felt. I would later learn about a term called "skin hunger." I was hungry for love and attention, but not the kind he had in mind. Had I known then what I know now, I would have gotten up and ran out of the building, but I didn't. I just knew it felt good.

The more I talked about my pain, the more he kept massaging my leg. As his hand continued to crawl up my leg, I chose to keep talking. I was scared and didn't know what to do. I began to reason in my mind that he was just an affectionate person, and his hand felt good. But when he touched my private parts, I jumped. I really didn't understand what was happening to my body. Heat was spreading through my limbs, as his touch grew more intense. I was getting scared. However, he acted as if he wasn't doing anything out of the ordinary and encouraged me to keep talking as he continued to ask me personal questions.

What started off gentle soon began to get rough. I was afraid. I told him to stop. I tried to move his hand but I couldn't. He was stronger than I was, and he told me to relax and trust him. I tried, but he was hurting me. Eventually, he stopped but not without urging me to have my whole body dedicated to the Lord. He told me if I had my body dedicated, I could prevent bad things from happening. I didn't know what having my whole body dedicated to the Lord really meant but I said "No." In my mind, I reasoned that I was *never* going to get the Holy Ghost so I decided to get a job instead.

## MISSING THE BUS

Times were hard, and I was determined to help my mom out. I decided to get a job. Someone told me of a place where I could get a summer job. Being the independent type, I called directory assistance, got information from the bus station, and set out on my conquest. It probably would have helped if I knew which direction. Not one given to detail, I figured I would just ask the bus driver.

As I was making my way to the bus stop, I saw a bus pulling up on the opposite side of the road. I remember thinking, *I hope that's not my bus*, as I was too far away to catch it. A well-dressed gentleman who had stopped at a red light was playing gospel music. Hesitantly, I approached his car and asked him for direction. As I feared, he pointed in the opposite direction—the direction of the bus I had just missed. With a big sigh I said, "Thank you," and proceeded to cross the street.

After crossing the street, I looked over the bus schedule and sighed again. It would be another hour before the next bus came. I sat down and prepared to wait. To my surprise, the same gentleman I had previously asked for directions pulled up to the curb and asked me if I needed a ride. He said he was going the same way and did not mind dropping me off. Immediately, I heard the warning in my head to *never take a ride with a stranger*, but I ignored it. He looked like a nice man, and he was playing Christian music. It was hot, and I really didn't want to wait for the next bus, so I said yes.

As we drove, he began to engage me in light chatter. He told me he was a deacon in his church and asked me my name and age. He told me I was pretty and asked me if I had a boyfriend. I said, "No, of course not," blushing under his observation. I had no idea where we were or how far I was from my destination. I simply trusted that he was going to take me there.

After a few minutes of quiet time, he told me he needed to stop by a friend's house before he dropped me off. Innocently and unsuspectingly, I agreed. He started driving in and out of different alleys looking for his friend's house. He said it was the only way he could remember where his friend lived because it was dark the last time he went. Still being very chatty, I never questioned his actions.

As he stopped in the middle of one alley, I waited for him to get out. Instead, he turned to me and asked me to give him a kiss. I looked at him like he'd lost his mind. He said,

"*What you're not going to give me no kiss?*"

"*No.*" I replied.

He pulled out a knife and pointed it to my throat as he commanded me to move over closer and give him a kiss. Fear filled my body as I began to move closer. I was scared—very scared—but I complied. I didn't know exactly where I was, but I knew it was somewhere near Watts. The alley was empty—not a single person in sight.

I wanted to scream but the knife pointing towards my throat prevented me. If I tried to run, I didn't know where I could go. I was lost. I thought about the possibility of him killing me and was saddened because I knew no one would even know I was dead. I wished I had never taken that stupid ride! I began to pray. I was so afraid.

As he pulled my mouth to his, he began to grunt. He kissed me very roughly as he forced his tongue down my throat. I wanted to throw up. Still holding the knife next to my throat, he started unbuttoning my blouse—fondling each breast before he placed his mouth on them. As he began to unbutton my pants, I knew what was coming next. I pretended I was not there and started talking. When he finished, I told him Jesus loved him and would forgive him if he asked Him to. He was shocked and asked me what I'd said. I repeated myself. Then he asked me where I went to church. I told him the name of my church, and gave him the name of my pastor. He then said that he would drop me off in front of the building as he promised. I was glad that he didn't cut me. I was afraid of dogs, and now I was afraid of alleys too.

When we got to the building, I was shaken but I was still determined to go inside. He asked for one more kiss before I got out. I suppressed my tears as I turned and went inside the building. I was so glad to be alive that I literally ran inside. Once inside I froze; the company wasn't hiring at that time but gave me an application anyway. I took the application and left.

As I rode the bus home, I felt dirty. I was growing weary of the lustful stares men continually imposed on me. Looking out of the window, I saw a man give me a wink and make a lewd comment. My stomach literally turned. I wanted to scream, *"Stop looking at me like that!"* but I repressed the feeling and went home.

During this time, there was a lady in the church whom I admired greatly; she was the pastor's wife. She could sing and she could preach. She had a very strong voice, and she walked with a lot of authority. I wanted to be like her. I was drawn to her strength. I decided I was going to tell somebody. My mother was at work and my siblings were outside playing. At my weakest moment, I picked up the phone and decided to call the pastor's wife.

*"Hello."*

*"Hello, First Lady. This is Shari."*

Very warmly she replied, *"Well, hello Shari. I received your card in the mail and I want you to know I purchased a pair of earrings with the money you sent me. I'm actually wearing them right now."*

My little spirit just soared. For a long time, I wanted to do something nice for her so I had saved up my allowance, bought a card, and placed my money inside. It wasn't much but I felt really proud. For a few seconds, I could hardly speak. She was really somebody in my eyes and I was happy that she liked me. Nervously, I swallowed and paused wondering whether I should tell her or just hang up.

*"So, what's on your mind?"*

I decided to take the risk.

*"Actually there is something I want to tell you. This afternoon I took a ride from a stranger and he hurt me."*

*"What do you mean you took a ride? Did you try to run away?"*

*"No ma'am."*

*"Did you scream for someone to help you?"*

*"No ma'am."*

*"Did you cry?"*

I had learned years ago that crying does no good. This time I replied very hesitantly.

"*No ma'am.*"

"*Well then you must have enjoyed it!*"

I was shocked. How could she say that? I didn't know what to do, so I hung up as I accepted the blame. I already felt dirty, and now I felt guilty. It was my fault. She was right. I accepted a ride from a stranger. How stupid could I have been? Therefore, I shouldn't start looking for sympathy now.

That's all I needed for my internal critic to shift into overdrive again:

"*That's right, Shari. You are so stupid, and you did deserve it! You were the one who didn't want to wait on a bus. Now look what it got you.*"

The voices in my head were merciless. I didn't know how to turn them off or how to defend myself from these horrible accusations. My self-esteem continued to plummet, as I tried to defend myself from myself.

Beginning to cry, I fought back:

"*But I didn't know. Honestly, I thought he was a good, Christian man. He was playing Christian music. He said he was a deacon. I didn't think he would try to hurt me.*"

The internal conversation continued:

"*But didn't the pastor tell you if you didn't have your body dedicated to the Lord something evil was going to happen?*"

"*Yes, but I was afraid. I didn't want him to remove my clothes and touch me like that again.*"

"*You are so scary. Don't go looking for pity when something bad happens. You should have listened to him.*"

I felt so dirty and ashamed. I decided to take a bath. Everything was my fault. If only I had dedicated my body like my pastor had said maybe this would not have happened. Agreeing with the voices in my head, I finally gave in to self-pity and depression. I sat in the tub until the water grew cold trying to scrub away the shame. I found a very prim outfit, covered my body the best I could, and went to church.

It was midweek prayer and Bible study. Thank God for midweek services. Back then, we used to open the service by praying on our knees. I remember going to the front bench and weeping. I confessed my sins. Then I prayed hard. I wanted God to forgive me and cleanse me one more time.

After service, the pastor offered to take me home. He said his wife had explained to him what happened, and he wanted to talk to me. We drove in silence for a while before he began to speak.

*"My wife told me you called."*

I didn't say anything. I just looked straight ahead.

*"She also told me what happened."*

He placed his hand on top of my thigh and began to rub my leg.

*"Why don't you move over here a little closer and tell me what happened."*

As I shared the details, his hand found a resting place under my skirt. Instead of taking me home, he drove behind the church my grandfather had previously rented out to him. No one was there as he parked behind the building. He told me to lie down and he would make everything better. He said he was going to make me feel better, but I did not feel better. I felt worse. When he finished pleasuring himself with me, something inside of me broke. He dropped me off at home and feelings of repulsion welled up inside of me. I hated him. I hated me. I hated life. I remember going into the kitchen and grabbing a butcher knife. I opened up the back door and sat outside with the butcher's knife in my hand. That night, for the very first time, I tried to take my own life.

Why? I was tired of feeling helpless. I was tired of feeling as if I had no control. I hated being made to do things I did not want to. I had no one to talk to and no place to hide. My mom was never around, my older sister and brother were living in their own worlds, and my younger sisters were too young to understand what was going on. I hated the way I felt. I hated my life.

Making incisions on my wrist, I remember looking up to heaven and thinking, *I can't take this anymore.* I kept asking God to take my life, but to no avail. It was not God's will for me to die, but that did not prevent me from trying.

# HELP MOMMY HELP

*Mommy, Mommy where are you?*
*How I wish I could come and talk to you.*
*Mommy, Mommy I know you really care,*
*But tonight I need you to show me*
*Because tonight I'm really scared.*

*Mommy, I know you think I'm strong, fearless and brave*
*And nothing gets to me*
*But it's only a mask I wear*
*To cover my insecurities and pain*
*Because deep down inside I actually feel*
*Lonely, Naked and Ashamed.*

*Oh Mommy, how I wish you would hold me*
*And tell me everything is going to be okay.*
*Your words would bring such healing*
*And help me through this awful pain.*
*But you're not here it's only a dream*
*And now it's time for me to get up and face reality.*

For the next few years, I continued to have meetings with my pastor. I think he believed he was helping me and could not grasp how much he was hurting me. From the sixth to the eighth grade, he found ways to meet with me. Sometimes he would pick me up from school and drop me off around the corner as school let out. Often he would find ways to take me home from church. There were others, but somehow he always managed to drop me off last. I began to ditch school a lot and isolated myself from my peers.

For a while, I really believed this was my lot in life. No one ever questioned my actions or my whereabouts. I didn't have a lot of friends. I had one best friend in the sixth grade, but she told me she had to get a new friend because I was never there. That's because early on I figured out how to avoid having the attendance office call my home when I was absent. I realized that I could miss two days and return on the third day without them calling home and notifying my mom. So in the morning I would get dressed like I was going to school, but as soon as the coast was clear, I would return home. Often I used to hide on the side of the house, or in the playhouse, where no one could see me.

I hated what was going on but eventually I began to accept it. In my heart I wanted so much to trust this preacher, but there was so much I didn't understand. I didn't understand how something could feel so good one moment and then hurt so bad the next. I used to beg him to stop as I would try to move his hand off my leg and pull my dress back down, but it didn't do any good. He was stronger than I was, and no amount of pleading would make him stop once he got into a certain groove. As the heat spread through my limbs, my mind would often leave my body as I pretended I was somewhere else. I would talk about anything and everything to escape what I knew was coming next.

At one point, I tried to tell the other church members what was going on, but they didn't want to hear it. They told me we were not supposed to talk about the pastor like that. If there was something I saw that I didn't like, I was supposed to pray about it. So that's exactly what I did. I started singing and moaning like the older members did. I really didn't understand some of those songs, but I did find comfort. I also found out God does hears and answer prayers. As I was coming home from a midweek Bible session one night, He made his presence very real to me.

### Divine Intervention

I remember that night as if it was yesterday. I was returning home from mid-week Bible study riding in the church van with a few saints who had decided to carry the prayer meeting from the church to the van. That is, they were singing, praying, clapping their hands, and praising God just as they did in church. I sat in the front wishing they would be silent long enough for me to figure out what I was going to wear to school the next day, but they didn't stop. They continued singing and praying all the way to my house.

Suddenly, under the anointing of the Holy Spirit, one of the sisters placed her hands on my shoulder. I felt a surge of electricity shoot through my whole body. My body felt like a light bulb. Somehow *I knew* I was in the presence of God. I could literally feel the power of God flowing through my being, starting at the top of my head all the way down to my toes!

Speaking under the power of the Holy Ghost I could hear the sister say, "*You are a chosen vessel before the Lord!*" As she spoke, I could feel oil being poured over my head. It literally felt like someone had placed me under a spout of oil and I could feel it as it ran down my head to my clothes. Then, as if someone would dim a light switch, the brightness began to fade and I was back with the saints.

Dazzled by what had just taken place, I looked toward the sister who had given me that word. She was just rejoicing and praising God. She then gave me a big hug and encouraged me to hold on because God had some big things in store for me.

As I walked into the house that night, I knew my life would forever be altered. I didn't know how or when, but I began to dream of doing something great for God. God himself had touched me and anointed me with oil. I felt special. I felt loved. No longer did I feel alone. I felt as if I had hope; hope that one day things would change. And change they did—just not exactly the way I'd envisioned.

"For I know the plans I have for you," declares the LORD,
"Plans to prosper you and not to harm you,
Plans to give you hope and a future".
(Jer. 29:11 NIV)

# A CHANGE IS COMING

In the midst of all of this, my mom had met a man to whom she was growing closer to everyday. One day she made an announcement that rocked our world. She called us all in the room and announced that she was getting married and we were all moving to a new city.

My mother explained how she was getting older and needed somebody to be with her after we were all grown. She said she was tired of the struggle of raising six children alone and that we should be grateful that she had found a man who was willing to take her with all of her children. We were not grateful. We hated the idea and protested, but all the protesting and complaining in the world wouldn't change my mommy's mind.

My new stepdad had a six-bedroom house built for his new bride, parked a brand-new car in her driveway, and ordered new appliances for the house. He even cooked and cleaned. As far as she was concerned, he was an answer to her prayers!

The marriage and move took place right before I turned fifteen. I was transferred to a new school, and I acquired two new sisters in the process. Prior to the transfer, my mom had petitioned the school board and arranged for me to be bused. No longer was the pastor able to touch me as I went to school now forty miles away from the city. God also supplied a way for me to be taken home from church by one of the members who lived nearby. Visits in his office were greatly reduced as a result.

Several months after the move, as I walked home from school, I noticed a car following me. My heart froze with fear as I realized whose car it was. *It was the pastor's car!*

As he pulled up behind me, he told me to get in the car and took me for a drive. Something inside of me snapped that night; I made up my mind that it would be the last time he would ever touch me. I decided to write a letter. I didn't know who I was going to give it to, and I didn't care, all I knew was I had to write.

With a determination I had never felt before, I freed my soul on paper. I wrote down everything—all the things that I wanted to say but had been too scared. For once I didn't care what anyone thought. I didn't care that I wasn't supposed to talk about the pastor, or if what I was writing was inappropriate. I wrote what I felt. I wrote until all the anguish, all the fear, and all the hatred I had carried around for years was released. I wrote the truth, then I addressed the letter to his wife.

Placing the pen down, I read the letter and realized I couldn't go through with this—unless I pretended that I was getting advice for someone else. Then no one would accuse me.

Taking great pains to erase my name and insert "a friend" in its place, I felt lighthearted. I had freed my soul on paper and exposed the source of my pain. However, before going to school, that next day I had second thoughts. The thought of someone actually reading this letter was too much for me to bear. Cowering in fear, I placed the letter in my robe and tucked my emotions safely back into my heart. As far as I knew, no one else knew and no one cared anyway. In a moment of weakness I had lashed out, but now the real world was staring me in the face. Dismissing the notion as silly, I quickly put it out my mind and went to school never thinking about that letter again.

I don't know when, but somehow Mommy found the letter and gave it to the pastor's wife. Looking back now, I wish she had talked to me first. I wish I had known how furious she was. I wish I could have seen her grab her gun and sit in front of his house waiting for him to come home so she could kill him. I wish I knew how the pastor's wife begged my mom not to kill her husband. I wish I could have heard how she ultimately convinced mom not to do it by reminding her that there would be no one to take care of her children as she rotted in jail. I wish I could have understood that her silence was not her way of rejecting me, but simply demonstrated a lack of knowledge of how to help me. I wish I had known then what I know now. Maybe things would have worked out differently. *But that is not how it happened...*

## THE SECRET IS OUT

Late one Saturday night, I received a phone call from the pastor's wife, who was less than friendly. Her words were curt. With no formal greeting she went straight to the point: *"Why didn't you tell me?"*

It only took me a second to figure out who she was and what she was talking about. I couldn't respond. I was frozen with fear. In that second, I knew she knew.

*"Why didn't you tell me he was doing this to you?"*

*"Tell you what?"*

*"I think you know what I'm talking about."*

I could hear the steel in her voice. My blood felt cold as she went on.

*"Maybe I should just move out of my house so you can have my bedroom too."*

I was shocked. I couldn't believe what I was hearing.

*"I never wanted your husband."*

I somehow managed to get out. She sounded so mean, so cruel, and so harsh. Nothing like the lady I had painted her to be. Yet, her opinion of my actions meant so much to me. I was crushed.

How could she think I wanted her husband? I never told her because I didn't want to hurt her. I didn't want her to know what her husband was doing. I never meant to hurt her. I was heartbroken, as she went on the tears began to flow. My role model no longer respected me and this knowledge left me reeling. As I turned to hang up the phone, my mother's face appeared. Her voice was low but her words clear as she asked,

*"How could you do that to her?"*

In my mind, the decision was unanimous: *they both believed it was my fault!*

I ran to my room. My face was burning as hot tears began to flow. I shut the door, fell on the floor, and wept as one question after another whirled in my mind.

- *How could she say that?*
- *What did he tell her?*
- *How did she find out?*
- *Who told my mom?*

As her words reverberated in my mind, I couldn't stop crying. I hated myself. I wished I had never written that stupid letter. Now everything is my fault. Crying out to God, I began to plead my case. I never intended to hurt anyone. I just wanted him to stop hurting me. *Why was I being blamed?*

The tears continued to flow. I cried over innocence lost. I cried for the first time he ever touched me. I cried for my unheard pleas. I cried for me.

*"Oh God, I never meant to hurt anyone. I never meant for it to get out, honestly."*

Then I grew angry. Why did he ever have to touch me anyway? Why couldn't he have just prayed when I went up to the altar to receive the Holy Ghost? I began to plead with God.

*"Honestly God, I just wanted you. I just wanted the gift of the Holy Ghost. I didn't know Lord. Oh God, what have I done?"*

Resignation began to set in. Life was cruel, and I was sick of being misused. I cried until I couldn't cry anymore. Feeling as if I was holding my heart in my hands, the tears finally subsided long enough for me to be still before the Lord. And that's when I realized—God *wasn't blaming me!*

What a revelation. I felt so much relief and joy! Somewhere deep down inside, I knew God was not blaming me and with that knowledge came peace. I didn't understand all the dynamics of what was going on, but I knew He did and that knowledge was enough to give me comfort as I finally fell asleep.

*"When his people pray for help,*
*He listens and rescues them from their troubles"*.
(Ps. 34:17 CEV)

## DECEIVED!

After that night, something on the inside of me broke and I didn't know how to fix it. My self-image had been attacked greatly. I felt unwanted, lost, and rejected. With no one to talk to, I grew progressively worse. I knew God. I knew He had chosen me to carry His word, to be an example among my peers, and to make a difference. He had touched my life and filled me with an awareness of His existence and love. I had received a charge, and I knew it.

Yet, I was suffering from hurt and rejection, and I took it out on Him. I couldn't understand why I had to experience so much suffering and pain when all I wanted to do was please Him. I used to dream about traveling the world to share the good news. Now miles away from the only community I had ever known, I felt ostracized by the very people I was trying to protect. What's worse is I believed they all thought it was my fault. Why else would they blame me? Why didn't anyone ask me what really happened? Not even once was the subject brought up.

For a while, I tried to fight the self-loathing thoughts, which plagued me constantly, but I couldn't because deep down inside I really did believe it was my fault. Why else would they say that? I tried to pray, but there were so many things I didn't understand. I didn't know how to fight all of the negative thoughts bombarding my mind. I was left to fend for myself. And that's exactly what I did. It was a new day, and I was determined to ditch this church girl stuff.

For me, that meant no more Bible studies, prayer meetings, street witnessing, singing in the choir, or church speeches. Although I loved experiencing the presence of God, I decided it was just too painful to serve Him. *I had been accused of trying to destroy a marriage and sleep with the pastor, and I had believed it was my fault.*

Looking back now, I can see that more than anything, I was just looking for a way to numb the pain, and that meant church avoidance. I felt rejected and I was looking for somewhere to fit. I was tired of always being on the outskirts. I was ready to see what it was like to fit in, and the adversary had his team in position, ready to attack. Therefore, there was only one thing left to do: quit walking with God. If only I could have realized how much Satan hated me, I would never have walked away from the one who loved me most.

For example, when my mom married my step dad, I got two stepsisters. One stepsister and I were the same age. We attended the same high school. There was a slight difference in the two of us. While I had spent my time in church, she had spent hers in the streets learning. She knew how to dress, how to talk, and how to walk with confidence. As far as clothing was concerned, she had all the right gear. She knew how to style her hair and wasn't afraid to take chances.

I later learned that she was carrying a deep pain in her heart because of the death of her mother. She had been unable to comprehend why God had allowed her mother to be diagnosed with cancer, and then die (especially when she had confessed scriptures pertaining to healing). It had taken its toll on my new stepsister and caused her to become bitter against God. Why didn't He heal her as He did the people in the Bible?

With bitterness came resentment, which was directed mostly toward my mom as well as all the people who told her that her mom died because she didn't have enough faith. Adding misery to pain, my stepsister was suddenly part of a new family with many new brothers and sisters. She was raised as an only child for over ten years, and it was hard for her to adjust. Even when her baby sister arrived, there was such a big age difference between the two. My stepsister had grown accustomed to having her way and controlling her dad. As far as she was concerned, my mother had stolen her dad, and she was determined to get her back. This she would do by making mom's life miserable. That's where I came in.

We were always being compared, and for a while, she came up short. Therefore, when I decided to walk away from God and began to seek ways to become accepted in the wrong crowd she was ready to oblige. The first thing we did was meet the boys.

### Boy, Boys, Boys!

We had so many coming over to our house that my step-father finally put his foot down and said we could only have visitors on Tuesdays and Thursdays. Of course we found a way around that by began sneaking out of the house and cutting classes so we could hang out with the wrong crowd.

There were two girls in particular that took a strong liking to me. These were the type of girls I normally would've avoided like the plague. Their life represented everything I had been taught to avoid. They were involved in some bad stuff. Yet in my struggle to feel accepted, I chose to hang out with them. They taught me how to smoke, steal, party, get high, and encouraged me to engage in sex. When I consider all the ditching, stealing, getting high, and sleeping around I did, it is a wonder I ever passed the tenth grade!

Going against my conscience was hard, and deep down inside it was a cry for help. Sometimes at the end of the day, I would tally all the things I stole and just cry because I was miserable inside. The fires of God had touched my soul, yet I was continuously doing everything I knew to be ungodly.

As the days progressed into months, my mom noticed the change in my behavior and began to question my actions. One day she pulled me aside and earnestly rebuked me. She told me she always thought I was the strong one, but pointed out that instead of me pulling my stepsister to Christ, my stepsister was pulling me away.

Though I knew what she said was true, I wasn't ready to hear her. I was hurt, angry, and acting out of my pain. I had made my decision, and for the time being, I was determined to carry it out. I had made a vow that I would never let anyone hurt me like this again. I was going to be in control of my life. I would never be at the mercy of another man again. If something happened, it would be because I allowed it, not because I was being forced or threatened. I would decide whom, when, and where. I am so glad I serve a God who is able to look past our faults and see our pain. Someone once told me if a baby is crying, find out why before you get upset. Nine times out of ten dealing with the problem will make the crying stop.

Although I had chosen to walk away from God, He had not walked out on me (thank you God). He sent me two young believers who attended my new high school. They were not ashamed of Christ. God used them both in their own uniqueness to reach me. I loved the way the way they carried themselves. They walked with confidence, as if they owned the world. I knew something was different about them the first time I met them. They had a light on the inside that drew me to them. For a season, I spent some time getting to know both of their families. We didn't live too far from each other. They chose not to hang out with me, but to pray for me. They showered me with love, acceptance, and encouragement. I envied both of them in different ways, but not enough to change. I was not ready to commit my life back to the Lord yet, but I admired them from a distance. Later on, God would use the seed He had allowed to be planted by them to play a significant role in my life.

I spent the better part of the next two years distancing myself from anything that resembled church or pain. My stepsister and I had our birth certificates falsified, and I landed my first job inside a snack bar at a local department store. Often assigned to the register, I quickly learned how to help myself to the money without getting caught. Later I advanced to stealing clothes, jewelry, and shoes, all in an effort show how cool I really was. I would often pick up a few things for my new friends also.

After being warned that a security guard was monitoring my actions, I decided to take a job in the mall. That's where I meet my first real boyfriend. He was a junior in college. We used to work in the same shoe store. He was an educated college boy who wasn't afraid to speak his mind. One day, I heard him spewing out his beliefs about God in the store. My interest was piqued, but not for long. In my opinion, his beliefs were off, and worst of all he seemed to be influencing others. I was appalled.

Even though I was not living the lifestyle of a Christian, I still felt it was my duty to point out the error of his logic (according to the Bible). He was impressed with my knowledge and asked me out. I agreed to go out with him to get him saved. The only problem was he wasn't looking to get saved, and before long he began to influence me.

We started dating. I used to love the way he showered me with expensive gifts and took me out to eat at fancy restaurants. He even allowed me to drive his brand-new, fully-loaded, T-top Camaro. That was a big deal for a sixteen year old, and he didn't mind showing me a good time. The only problem was I didn't love him, and when I tried to break it off he became possessive, which caused him to do some frightening things.

The turning point came one evening after returning from the Ambassador Hotel. A couple that appeared to be the happiest and most beautiful couple I had ever seen had mesmerized me. Although I was wearing an expensive dress, complete with matching accessories, I felt empty inside. It was obvious to me that they were in love. She looked so happy and content although outwardly they seemed to be poor.

Something about their self-abandonment touched something deep in me. Here I was living in a six-bedroom house, wearing all the right stuff, dating a man who was my senior, and I felt empty inside. I couldn't explain it, but watching them sparked a desire inside me for something I thought I had long since buried—*love.*

Arriving home later that night, I remembered the modest yet happy couple as I opened my closet and took a quick surveillance of all the clothes, shoes, and material things I had acquired. I was overwhelmed with feelings of loneliness and emptiness.

*Was this all life was about? Acquiring more and more stuff?*

All I had done was try to bury the pain with money, drugs, and sex. I had pretended not to care, but the pain was still there. This realization triggered an emotional response that left me reeling. *Oh God, what have I done?*

All the feelings I had buried from the past resurfaced, and for a second all I could see was a scared little girl surrounded by all of the men who had abused her. Backing up into a corner, I kneeled on the floor and began to curl up and wrap my arms around myself in fetal position. I could see the men coming towards me from all directions. As if trying to hide, I began to feel my mind leave my body. At this moment, the sound of a phone ringing snapped me back to reality. Grabbing it quickly, I answered.

*"Hello."*

*"What's wrong?"*

It was my friend from high school calling (the one I had secretly admired and envied). It had to be almost 3:00 a.m. I wondered what had made her call at that moment. She began to explain that the Lord woke her up out of a dead sleep and told her to call. All I could do was cry as I tried to explain what was wrong. I'm sure I was not making much sense but she knew she needed to pray. That's exactly what she did. I could see the men retreating and sensed my mind returning with each word spoken.

After the prayer, she insisted that I come over to her house right then. She didn't have to tell me twice. I had to get out of that room. Arriving at her house in the wee hours of the morning she gave me her bed and she slept on the floor. I felt safe. She told her mom and they went into intercession for me. The next day I broke up with my boyfriend, and before the week was over, I rededicated my life to Christ. I could finally see that hanging out with the popular crowd had only produced seeds of destruction in my life. I had learned how to fit in by doing all the things I said I never would. Trying to fit in had cost me my self-respect, and I no longer felt good about myself. I was a backslider and I knew it. God had called me to preach, and I had failed Him miserably. It was time to turn my life around.

## THE TURN AROUND

*You know there is one thing I have learned about God. He knows how to get your attention!*

God got my attention one night at a dinner party held in the home of my friend's relative. Unbeknownst to me, I had a divine appointment as I was about to meet my new pastor-to-be. The dinner party was being held in his honor. He was leaving his current ministry and transitioning to pastoral ministry.

I walked in on a conversation already in progress and immediately voiced my opinion (which was in direct opposition to what I was hearing). The evening progressed with little quips from me over dinner. After dinner, the young pastor pulled out his King James Bible and began to read the following verses:

*There is no fear in love; but perfect love casteth out fear because fear hath torment. He that feareth is not made perfect in love. We love him because he first loved us. If a man says, I love God, and hateth his brother, he is a liar: for he that loveth not his brother who he hath seen, how can he love God whom he hath not seen?*

1 John 4:18–20

Unaware that the scripture was not open for debate I responded, *"I can love God and hate my brother, because God would never treat me the way my so-called brother has."*

Instantly the room grew silent as the others stared at me in amazement. With the patience of Job, the young pastor began to explain why my thinking was incorrect. The problem was that I saw nothing wrong with my thinking and took offense that he did!

A heated discussion followed. As far as I was concerned, he was obviously wrong and someone needed to enlighten him. After a few minutes of going back and forth, my friend's mother, filled with the wisdom of God, interjected a thought into the discussion.

*"What if your brother has wronged you?"*

As if someone had just whispered a secret in his ear, the young pastor looked at me and said in a voice filled with compassion, *"I know what happened."*

At the time, I was not familiar with the gifts of the spirit, and I had no understanding about the word of knowledge or prophecy, but somehow I just knew that he knew. Treading very gently, he asked if the group could pray with me. My first thought was to get up and run out of the room. My big secret was out and the only thing I wanted to do was hide. Why? Because deep down I still believed it was all my fault!

Unable to run or hide, my pride kicked in. I was not about to break down in front of this group and my pride would not allow me to show any signs of vulnerability or weakness.

Therefore, I simply shrugged and said, "Sure." A chair was placed in the middle of room. I sat as the saints began to encircle me with prayer. Not understanding what just happened or even why I dismissed myself as soon as they finished praying. I secretly prayed that I would never see that minister again. That would not be the case. In light of the fact that I had rededicated my life to Christ and revealed some of the scars to my friend, one day she invited me to church where this young minister now preached. I didn't want to look bad in front of her family, so I agreed to go.

The meeting was held in a small room behind a larger church. The atmosphere was warm, friendly, and inviting, so I decided to return with my friend that evening. At the close of the meeting, the young pastor made an altar call and I responded. After the prayer, he requested we each turn and greet our neighbor with a hug as we dismissed.

I can't explain it, but somehow something on the inside of me broke once more. The vow I made as a child resurfaced as I remembered all of the hurt I had endured in church. Tears began to run down my face as I quickly reached for the door. Pausing long enough to remember I was leaving my friend, I turned around, and to my amazement, there stood the pastor directly in front of me. Reaching out for my shoulders, he began to say over and over again: *"No one is going to hurt you here….No one is going to hurt you here."*

Unable to believe the word of the young pastor, I looked toward his wife. She had a very serene disposition, and she was nodding her head back and forth in complete agreement. I finally calmed down long enough to listen and agreed to come back.

This began my entrance back to church. It was a small church located in a poor area. Prior to this, I had visited a very large church with thousands of members. This small church, on the other hand, resembled a storefront with less than twenty members. Yet this was the place God had chosen to begin a series of healings in me. The first lesson on the agenda was love.

> *"Beloved let us love one another: for love is of God;*
> *and every one that loveth is born of God and knoweth God.*
> *He that loveth not knoweth not God;*
> *for God is love".*
>
> 1 John 4:7–8

For one solid year, this young pastor preached on love. He laid a foundation explaining in depth that God loves us. No matter the mistakes and failures of our past, God wanted to bring us back into relationship with Him, heal our hurts, and fill us with His love.

Unable to comprehend the magnitude of love God had for me or the love his people had for me, I decided to test the waters. On many occasions, I left the meeting abruptly as the minister began to teach, slamming the door loudly to announce my exit. However, once in the car, I would often cry as I tried to make sense of what I just heard. I was still very much wounded and extremely guarded, and unfortunately I gave that young group of believers something to pray about!

No matter how badly I treated some of the members, especially the pastor and his wife, they continued to reach out to me in love (not that funny kind of stuff but real agape love). Often they invited me to their house for food and fellowship. I began to warm up to them, and slowly I began to feel accepted in this crowd. With a lot of patience and love, they encouraged me to accept the love of God and the love they freely offered. It took a lot of prayer, fasting, soul searching, and a desire to be free for me to change, but after a year, I slowly began to open up and learn how to receive love.

*The revelation that God was not holding me accountable for the things I had done but had placed my sins on His Son was life-changing. By accepting the atonement offering of Christ, I had been declared not guilty! And the best news was He still wanted to use me!*

I finally was ready to change. I wanted to receive the knowledge and the power to overcome sin. At last I was ready to submit to the Holy Spirit. Hence began lesson number two: *forgiveness.*

# FORGIVENESS

*Then came Peter to Him, and said, "Lord, how oft shall my brother sin against me, and I forgive him? Till seven times?" Jesus saith unto him: "I say not unto thee, until seven times: but, until seventy times seven." Therefore is the kingdom of heaven likened unto a certain king, which would take account of his servants. And when he had begun to reckon, one was brought unto him, which owed him ten thousands talents. But forasmuch as he had not to pay, his lord commanded him to be sold and his wife, and children and all that he had, and payment to be made. The servant therefore fell down, and worshipped him, saying, Lord, have patience with me, and I will pay thee all.*

*Then the lord of that servant was moved with compassion, and loosed him, and forgave him the debt. But the same servant went out, and found one of his fellow servants, which owed him an hundred pence. And he laid hands on him, and took him by the throat, saying, 'Pay me what thou owest.' And his fellow servant fell down at his feet, and besought him, saying have patience with me, and I will pay thee all. And he would not; but went and cast him into prison, till he should pay the debt.*

*So when his fellow servants saw what was done, they were very sorry, and came and told unto their lord all that was done. Then his lord, after he had called him, said unto him, 'O thou wicked servant, I forgave thee all that debt, because thou desiredst me. Shouldest thou not also have had compassion on thy fellow servant, even as I had pity on thee?" And his lord was wroth, and delivered him to the tormentors, till he should pay all that was due unto him.*

*So likewise shall my heavenly Father do also unto you, if ye from your hearts forgive not every one of his brother their trespasses.*

Matthew 18: 21–35

I placed my Bible down as the realization of what I just read hit me like a bomb. *God wanted me to forgive my offenders!*

Why would God want me to forgive the people who had ruined my childhood, especially my former pastor? He knowingly used my naïveté to rob me of my innocence. Then he covered his tracks under the guise of pastor/counselor. He pretended to help me receive the Holy Ghost and teach me how to be a better Christian when all the while he just wanted what was under my dress. *I was supposed to forgive him? No way!*

I was not ready to let it go. Someone needed to pay and I wanted this debt to be paid in full. Never mind that God had forgiven me, just like the king had forgiven his servant in the parable, I wanted my offender to pay back all!

However, I did not realize the Holy Spirit was trying to set me free. By holding on to the sins others had committed against me, I was tied to the very ones I wanted to be rid of. Why? Because *what you refuse to release, you will ultimately keep.*

I was miserable. I wanted to please God, but he was asking too much of me. To face, forgive, and release people who had wounded me deeply was more than I could take. This new direction the Holy Spirit was requesting me to take was unthinkable. As far as I was concerned, someone needed to pay for my pain and I was not going to let anyone off the hook. Crying out to God, I began to plead my case:

*"Oh God I can't. I just can't. Why would you make such an unreasonable request considering all that I have been through? You know my story. You saw what happened. You knew I was simply trying to please*

*you yet you let all of this stuff happen to me. Now you want me to forgive? I can't do this Lord!"*

Very calmly I heard the Holy Spirit say:

*"Yes you can."*

*"But God it's not fair. Someone needs to pay!"*

I began to battle with unforgiveness, self-hatred, depression, and anger for the rest of that year. Although I had rededicated my life back to Christ, I was still carrying wounds from the past and I couldn't see past my pain. I knew what the Holy Spirit wanted me to do but all I could think about was the hurt and pain caused by those who were supposed to love me and protect me.

Things I had buried for years began to resurface and I grew more and more stubborn. At the time I just couldn't see that my freedom would come from my obedience. My day in court finally came. God was requiring an answer from me.

- Would I forgive all the men who had hurt me?
- Would I forgive my parents who had forsaken me?
- Would I forgive God for allowing all of this evil to come into my world?
- Or would I continue to hold on to bitterness and resentment?

Christ had forgiven me. I had walked out on Him and committed all types of sinful acts that I knew were against His holy ordinance and yet He chose to forgive me. And now it was my turn.

Unable to bear the weight of convictions any longer, I finally picked up the phone and made an appointment to meet with my former pastor one Sunday after church. It was one of the hardest things I ever did. I chose to go alone and told no one of my intent.

As I made my way to the office, I asked the Lord to help me. Opening the door, I immediately saw his wife (the woman who had accused me of trying to take her husband) sitting valiantly by his side. As they sat behind the desk, I stated the reason for my visit. I had come to ask for forgiveness: for harboring hurt and anger against them. I then requested them to forgive me if I had caused them any pain. They both accepted my apology but offered none. We talked for a few minutes and then I left driving straight to my pastor's house. He could not believe what I had just done and told me how proud he was of me.

In the meeting that night, the Holy Spirit filled me with so much joy that I finally realized it didn't matter if they had requested me to forgive them or not. I was free, truly free, and I relished in that joy. My willingness to humble myself and follow the Holy Spirit's leading had given me the courage to face my enemies and forgive them. I now was experiencing a freedom I never had! Praise the Lord! At last the forgiveness test had finally been passed!

# The Big Cover Up

*Pain, Pain*
*I know pain*
*Because I like so many of you*
*Kept silent about the crimes*
*Committed in a little dark room.*
*It was our little secret*
*Or so I was told*
*When he began an invasion*
*That would taint my very soul.*

*Innocence ended*
*A tragedy for sure*
*But still I kept silent*
*And never said a word.*
*Fear had set in,*
*And I supposed he knew*
*I would never tell anyone*
*What happened in that little room.*
*Today I grieved*
*For the little girl*
*Who lost her virginity.*

*How I wished I knew*
*I could always come*
*And talk to you*
*But it seemed like*
*You w`ere never there.*
*Besides, deep down inside*
*I felt like I was to blame*

*And I didn't trust anyone*
*To understand the depth of my pain.*

*How many years*
*Have I longed to be free*
*From the tormenting pain of my*
  *childhood memories?*
*I tried to run.*
*I tried to hide.*
*I tried to bury the pain*
*Deep down on the inside.*

*I used to wonder*
*If you ever knew*
*What this would do to a child*
*Who placed her trust in you.*
*You were called to minister*
*"The gospel"*
*A message designed to set men free*
*Yet you took advantage*
*Of my naiveté*
*When you raped me*
*Of my virginity.*

*For years I walked around*
*Feeling like I was less,*
*Until I met the Savior*
*Who told me I was loved*
*And truly blessed!*

With loving kindness
He drew me out of a horrible pit
Showering me with His love,
Healing me from roots of bitterness.

He didn't turn His face away
Even though he could see
I was covered in shame.

On the contrary,
He reached out
His nailed-scarred hands to me
And broke the chains
That held me in captivity!

The chains of the past
Began to fade away
When He made his home
In my heart that day.
And more than anything
It was His Word
That truly set me free.
You see He has promised
That He will never leave
Neither will He ever forsake me

For the next few years, I faithfully attended services and applied my heart to learn the principles of love and forgiveness. It was a good church and I felt like I was adopted into the family. My family could not understand why I insisted on going to that little church, but I didn't care. I wanted to continue to experience the joy I had found in serving Christ, and this pastor seemed to have the wisdom of God. I became involved in the life of the church and the weights began to fall off one by one. It was now time for lesson number three: *holiness!*

*I beseech you therefore brethren by the mercies of God, that you present your bodies as a living sacrifice, holy, acceptable unto God, which is your reasonable service. And be not conformed to this world but be ye transformed by the renewing of your mind that ye may prove what is that good, and acceptable, and perfect will of God.*

Romans 12:1–2

Although I had released several of the people who had hurt me, I was in need of a new mindset. That is, I was used to calling my own shots, and the ways of the Spirit (or Christian living) did not always agree with my thinking. Therefore, if I could see the logic of, and happened to agree with, it I was more likely to obey than when I did not. Rather than submit, I would simply dismiss the notion (or command) as being ridiculous and continue doing what I thought was best.

For example, I had not yet learned how to *deny my flesh.* I still enjoyed having sex, drinking, dancing, and smoking. I learned all too well how to cover up. On Sundays, before pulling into the parking lot, I would always put my cigarettes out, turn down my *worldly music,* and hide any evidence of my dual lifestyle. But this little church was a holiness church, and they believed in living holy all the time. They actually had a little song they would sing from time to time: *Ride, ride don't let the devil ride. If you let him ride, he will want to drive.*

I would soon learn, through many tears and hard lessons, God's ways are not negotiable. *To walk with God you must learn to obey His word.* Even though God had a good plan for my life, learning to become submissive to His will for my life was a process that would take me many, many, many years to learn.

## THE COST OF DISOBEDIENCE

Mr. Personality, who could impress a crowd with his humor and wit, entered into my world during this season of compromise. We met at a Bible study. My friend's cousin was the leader of the group and had invited my friend and me to assist. Our first encounter was rocky, at best. He was a new babe in Christ and the group leader had been discipling him for a few months. Upon introducing him to the group, the leader shared that the new convert was a high school friend whom he'd recently had the privilege of leading to Christ.

Although this new addition to the Bible study was a babe in Christ, it was clear that he possessed a lot of natural and spiritual knowledge. He also displayed an admirable ability to easily and humbly share his heart. Humility was something I hadn't learned yet. It made me uncomfortable. I'd always thought of it as a sign of weakness. Being the competitive type, I felt a need to share my wealth of knowledge too! Primarily, I just wanted to show him he wasn't the only one that knew a thing or two, and when it was all over I was exhausted.

It would be five months before we would see each other again. In my opinion, the second meeting was worse. The leader of the Bible study was unable to teach one week, and asked if I would help out. I was honored. Arriving early, I soon realized my leader forgot to convey one small, yet important, fact: the Bible study was to be held at the home of Mr. Personality himself, and, to make matters worse, he'd asked Mr. Personality to teach the Bible study along with me!

The subject that night was love: *Demonstrating Brotherly Kindness One Toward Another.* It had been grueling, but I managed to suck it up and at least act congenial. After the meeting, one of the ladies needed a ride home. Upon hearing her plight, I offered to take her home, and, before I knew it, Mr. Personality offered to ride with me.

I was furious, but since I couldn't figure out how to say, "*No thank you, because I can't stand you*" in a nice, loving Christian way, I felt like I had no choice but to accept his offer.

After we dropped off our passenger, we stopped to get something to eat. I quickly discovered he had a hearty appetite although he was extremely thin. He ordered so much food that I threatened to leave him at the restaurant if he ordered one more thing. We then sat down and ate.

As the evening progressed, I slowly began to get over my initial dislike for the man. In fact, by the time we returned home, I knew Mr. Personality was a wonderful man with a vast amount of potential. I liked him a lot but, so did my good friend, and I didn't want to intrude on her territory. So after a few more weeks, we all sat down with the leader to discuss this situation. My friend graciously released him to me and we began to date.

However, it didn't take long before he began to notice we were not on the same page. In a very loving way, he told me although we were headed in the same direction, he could see we were taking two different roads to get there. Hence, he thought it best if we dissolved our relationship before we both got hurt. I refused. I thought we could work it out and insisted that we continue.

Someone once said addiction could be viewed as having relentless persistency in the wrong thing. That would be me. Like a bulldog grabbing on to a bone, I refused to let go.

I was not yet submitted to the process of sanctification. (That's where you deny your flesh; the unholy desires that loom in your mind and cause you to stray onto a forbidden pathway.) I practiced fleshly activity on a regular basis. Yet, instead of repenting for my sins, I would simply make excuses as to why it was okay for me to break the rules and indulge myself, as if spiritual laws and principles didn't apply to me. Expecting the Lord to make an exception for me, I simply overrode the warnings I perceived.

In other words, I was still in charge of my world (or so I thought). I called the shots. I did what I wanted, when I wanted, and was accountable to no one. I did not listen to, or submit to, counsel. This time, however, my pride and stubbornness would cause me great pain in the years to follow.

In all fairness, I knew we both had a lot of issues that needed some serious attention. I decided to help him with his, placing the work the Lord had started in me on the backburner, and work on him. I focused my time and energy on making him the man I thought he could be. Nothing was withheld. I gave him my car, my body, my time, and my money in exchange for his acceptance, approval, affection, and love.

Soon after Mr. Personality joined my church, I entered into an arena of social acceptance I had never experienced before in the church world. We were one of the young happening couples at my church and with that status came invitations to dinners, social events, and outings. My calendar was full. I was a college student, employed by a major aerospace company. I was young, I felt beautiful, and I was in love and engaged to be married. There was only one major problem: *I was not ready for marriage and neither was he.*

I knew that my self-esteem was not where it should be. I knew that I still had abuse issues that needed to be dealt with. My internal relationships with my mom and dad where still unresolved, and I had a major trust issue. However, none of that mattered. I was in love and for me that was all that mattered.

I ignored the warning signs the Holy Spirit continually showed me. We eventually got married, against the wishes of my family and close friends. The wedding went off without a hitch and off to our honeymoon we went.

## MARRIED, SEPARATED, DIVORCED

Life as a married woman was fun for the first year. We rented a small two-bedroom duplex. For the first month, we had no furnishings, not even a chair, but we were content because we were in love. Before long, my mother-in-law arranged to have a house full of furniture delivered; including a washer, dryer, and a little table for our breakfast nook.

We soon fell into a routine of married life. We both enjoyed entertaining, and we spent a lot of time surrounded by people. I enjoyed playing house, as I would prepare fancy meals, and he enjoyed being the life of the party.

For a season, I felt as if I married my boyfriend—only it included the benefit of sex without guilt. As long as we were socializing, everything was fine. However, the problems began to surface when we were left alone to face ourselves.

It wasn't long before I discovered that we had two different standards for living. I began to grow discontent with living on a budget. I wanted so much more out of life. Clothes, money, education, and fine dining were important to me, and I loved to hang out with the Jones' (people who had what I wanted). At the time, my mate worked part-time and seemed content as long as we had the essentials (rent, food, and clothing). He grew weary of my complaints, and I grew weary of trying to make him into the man I wanted him to be. We both had deep issues from our past that we had never dealt with, and when we were alone they began to surface. Feeling trapped, I started to gravitate toward food and church activities, and he began to gravitate toward drugs.

Life grew worse. Realizing the magnitude of the mistake I had made, I began to seek the Lord. I was in over my head, and I knew it. I didn't know how to deal with my mate being hooked on drugs, and I did a lot of pleading, begging, crying and nagging to get him to stop.

My handsome husband with the wonderful personality was drifting away slowly, and I did not know how to pull him back in. He was moving farther and farther away from God, his Christian friends, his family, and me. It was as if no one could reach him. I knew he hated disappointing everyone. He had so many unresolved issues, and deep inside, he was suffering from the pains of his past.

The pressure of trying to be there for everything and everyone overwhelmed him. When he was unable to live up to the facade, he chose to reach back to the world he knew instead of reaching out to God. With the drugs and booze came the pornography. My marriage was unraveling right before my face, and I didn't know how to fix it. The dream of living happily ever after was slowing fading, and each day I grew more and more depressed.

I seriously needed a break. We had a big social event sponsored by our church one night, and after it ended I decided to spend the night with a friend. I called my husband to let him know I wasn't coming home. The next morning I felt revived. I went to church and left service full of hope and anticipation. I had a sense that God was preparing me for something. You know that feeling you get when you know something is about to change, but you just aren't sure what it is. That's what I had. And since I was believing God to heal my marriage, I just assumed that God had somehow turned everything around—*not!*

I pulled up in front of the house, and I walked in, expecting to fall into the arms of my forgiving husband and make up. However, what I met was a man who looked like my husband, but sounded nothing like him. This one was crazed with anger and trying to hold onto his temper. The longer I looked, the more it seemed like I was looking into the eyes of a demon.

After a few minutes of listening to his tirade, I left the room quickly and reached for the keys. I was heading to the car when I realized it was time for me to stop running. I walked calmly back into the house and tried to reason with my husband as I watched him throw all of my belongings out of the closet. Fear set in as the realization of what he was doing and saying slowly began to pierce through my brain. *Was it really possible that our marriage was over?*

I didn't want to believe it was true. I walked to my friend's house and requested to use her phone. It was time to call home. My mom answered the phone and after speaking with her, I requested to speak to my older sister and told her the whole story as well. She immediately replied that she would be there right away.

In the meantime, my friend's husband and uncle went down to speak to my mate. What they found was a man out of control. Although my mate was extremely thin, it took both men to hold him down.

Eventually, my husband calmed down long enough to pack my car with my clothes and take it to my friend's house where he left the key. With the arrival of my sister, and the aid of my friend, I finally accepted the facts. My marriage was over.

I was unable to face my family just yet. I chose to go to church instead. Opening up one of the hefty bags, I pulled out a wrinkled dress and put it on. I'm sure I was a sight to see, as my appearance exemplified the way I felt. With puffy eyes, uncombed hair, and a wrinkled dress, I sat in church trying to put off the inevitable as long as possible. Deep down inside, I was hoping my husband would walk into the service and tell me everything was going to be all right. That scene never took place, and eventually I was forced to go back to my parents' house.

I drove around for another hour or two before I finally headed to my mother's house. It was late when I arrived home, and secretly I was very grateful that my sister had gone ahead and prepared the family and the extra bedroom for my arrival. The house was very quiet as I walked up the stairs and gently closed the door behind me. Dropping my bags to the floor, I stretched out on the bed in the dark and cried, as one question kept ringing over and over in my head: *Why did it have to end like this?* The truth is, it didn't.

As I looked for the answer, I discovered it was staring me right in the face. I had been unwilling to allow the Lord to finish the healing process He had begun in me. Despite all the warnings, I chose to give my heart to a man who betrayed me in a way I had not known was possible. Trying to run away from pain had just produced more!

I began to think back on the look on my mother's face when I told her I was getting married, as she tried to hide her hurt and disappointment. She, as well as my other family members, knew that I was making a terrible mistake, but I was resolved and there was little anyone could say or do. After our wedding, I had not visited my mom for almost nine months. She was hurt and didn't understand why I had cut her out of my life, but I was enjoying my independence and felt no need to explain.

I thought about all the abortions I had prior to getting married. The guilt and shame of knowing I had taken my children's lives almost killed me. Over the years, I had tried to bury the acts out of my consciousness but it only kept resurfacing time and time again. In my heart, I knew I was wrong, yet I kept trying to justify the act in my head. I had been overwhelmed with fear that my child would be abused like I had been. I would not even allow myself to consider the thought of becoming a parent. I just believed that I would be a single mom unable to provide a safe home for my child, because I would always be at work and forced to leave my child in the care of another.

The fears of having my child grow up as I had sent me straight to the abortion clinic over and over again. But in spite of all of that, I was still unwilling to stop having sex. You may wonder why. I will tell you: because my love tank was empty, and I had tried to fill it my own way. Now, I sat with a broken heart. I just wanted God to make everything better. Crying out to God just before falling asleep I prayed, *"Oh God, will you please just fix my marriage?"*

But God, who is infinitely wise, knew what I needed most was a revelatory (rhema) word. And that's exactly what He sent. Early the next morning, before daybreak, I heard these words spoken softly in my ear:

> *Lift up your heads, O ye gates! And be lifted up, you everlasting doors! And the King of glory shall come in. Who is this King of*

*glory? The Lord strong and mighty, The Lord mighty in battle.*
*Lift up your heads, O you gates! And lift them up, you everlasting*
*doors! And the King of glory shall come in. Who is this King of*
*glory? The Lord of hosts, He is the King of Glory.*

Psalm 24:7–10 (NKJV)

Three times I heard this verse repeated in my ear before I
woke up. That's when I realized it was the Lord! He had not
forsaken me nor abandoned me in my hour of need. In the
midst of my failure He had manifested His presence. *God had*
*sent His word to heal me!* As strength began to flood my soul, so
did waves of peace. Somehow I knew God was still in control,
and He was going to work everything out. Walking in a confidence I did not feel the night before, somehow I just knew
everything was going to be all right.

For the next few years, my husband and I lived apart. I signed
up for counseling classes and spent that time learning how to love
and forgive. It took the aid of three special counselors, loving
family members, friends, and a good church for me to understand
God's unconditional love, and the love of His people. I continued
to pray for the healing of my marriage until one day, I believed it
was time to go back home and give my marriage a second chance.

We moved in with his mother and stepdad. His stepdad
had been diagnosed with cancer and was slowly starting to fade
away. Leaving me to manage the house, my husband worked
and went to school. I stayed at home and learned how to be a
wife according to the word of God. That is, I learned how to
become submissive. Instead of trying to climb the corporate
ladder, I stayed at home and worked part time.

This time, instead of me seeking higher education, I helped
him pursue his degree. I learned how to pray. I learned how to

be a support to his mom and stepdad. It wasn't easy, but I was determined to get the lesson right this time.

For the next year, things went well until, one day, I noticed some of the old habits recurring. I resisted the temptation to run home this time. I prayed and I fought for our marriage. Yet no amount of pleading or prayer would persuade my husband to come to counseling with me.

Tired of hearing me cry and plead, one day the Lord did us both a favor. He allowed him to stop coming home. After a few months, he returned with this simple admission: He had gotten someone pregnant and thought it best if I heard it from him rather than someone else.

His admission left me reeling as my emotions plummeted downward. My world had revolved around him. I did not understand then what I know now: *it takes two healthy, whole, and willing participants to keep a marriage alive.* Although I had begun to make some significant strides through counseling to deal with my root issues, my mate was unwilling to face, process, and release his past at the time. Eventually he chose to walk away from God and me (his wife) and I responded vehemently,

*"What do you mean you got someone pregnant?"*

Tears flooded my face as I tried to digest the news. Unbelievable pain filled my heart as I looked into his eyes trying to comprehend the words he had just spoken. *"But…but I am your wife, and I have sacrificed everything to be with you."* My emotions were all over the place. What did he mean he had been with another woman, and he had gotten her pregnant? Wasn't I the one who encouraged him to go back to school? I cooked his meals. I washed his clothes. I waited for him to come home. Even when he was drunk or high, I still made love to him and this is how he repays me? He leaves me at his mother's house while he goes carousing with another woman!

A mixture of anger and grief filled my heart. Once again, it seemed that all the labor, all the prayers, all the sacrifices had seemingly been for naught. With anguish in my heart, I cried out to God.

*Oh God, Where are you? I can't take it anymore. Why God? Why did you let this happen? You could have stopped him. Didn't you hear my prayers? Didn't you see my tears? I begged him, I begged you, but still you let this happen to me.*

For the next few months, I walked through the valley of the shadow of death. If you have ever experienced a divorce, then you may know how painful it feels to have your heart ripped out of your chest. You don't feel like talking, eating, praying, or singing. Everything you once believed in is dead and you have been left to somehow pick up the pieces.

I would love to tell you I sailed though this season unblemished as I laid in the arms of Jesus, but that was not the case. Instead, I choose to drown myself in self-pity, isolation, rejection, loneliness, and fear. And when those feelings no longer medicated my pain, I began to harbor hurt and hatred in my heart until I actually started blaming God.

Feelings of isolation and rejection replaced the peace I once knew. I let my appearance go and turned to food for comfort. What a mistake! The more I ate, the worse I looked. I hated myself. I was lost and I knew it. I left the church for a season and picked up some of my old habits again.

Without spiritual accountability, or parental advice, I began to indulge more and more in immoral activities. *However, just because I had walked away from God again did not mean He had walked away from me*! My pastor was a praying man who believed in fasting and prayer as a lifestyle. Although I did not know it then, many members were praying and fasting for me. Many called, and others sent messages inquiring about my well-being, believing God for my safe return to the church. When I finally came to myself, I was received back into the fold with joy and thanksgiving.

*This is why I can speak as a living testimony. God's love for you is eternal and unconditional. He doesn't mind going to extreme measures to show you how much He loves you. After all, isn't that what His son's death on the cross is all about? Jesus Christ took your place for the sins you committed and those committed against you. God is not condemning you. On the contrary, He loves you, even when you don't love yourself. His hand is extended to you. The only thing you have to do is believe, receive, and accept His love and guidance.*

I had not learned that lesson yet. I chose to turn from the source of life and, very soon, I became like the woman at the well. No, I did not have five husbands, but, like the woman at the well, I started using men. And, this time, it was no holds barred.

## BRUISED, BITTER, AND MAD

Life had become bittersweet. I had lost my sense of purpose. I had lost my husband, and slowly I was losing my faith in God. Somehow I just felt like God had let me down. In my hour of greatest need, He failed to come through. I sincerely believed I had done all I could, and He failed me. I had stood on His word, confessed His word, slept with the word and believed His word. Yet, as far as I was concerned, He hadn't worked His word in my marriage. In the end, my marriage failed.

No longer trusting in God's ability, I threw caution to the wind as I started doing "my own thing" again. I continued to live with his mother for a nominal fee. Subconsciously, I think I was leaving the door open just in case my husband wanted to return, but in the end, he never did. I worked as a floater in a medium-sized office across town.

*I hated my life. I was hurt, bitter, angry, and disappointed with God.* I was in this state of mind when I met Mr. Money, a satanic snare from which it would take me two years to break free.

*"Good morning, Shari. Has anybody ever told you what a beautiful voice you have?"*

Immediately a smile came to my face. That was Mr. Money (he was the owner's very wealthy friend). I wasn't really sure what he did. I just knew he was exceptionally intelligent, drove a luxury car, and appeared to have a lot of money. I loved the way he spoke. He had exquisite taste and he walked with an air of confidence. Mr. Money had presence. His phone calls were always a pleasure to receive, because he always took time to make me feel good about myself. Today was no exception. Smiling, I responded.

*"Yes Mr. Money, how may I help you?"*

*"Well you could start by answering this question: How long are you going to keep making me carry this umbrella around?"*

*"What umbrella are you talking about?"*

*"For the last few months I've been trying to repay you for your services, and you keep giving me a rain check."*

Smiling inwardly I thought, *"How cute."* I had briefly assisted him with a project for the owner, and he wanted to take me out. However, I didn't think the owner would care for that and told him the same.

*"It's not that Mr. Money. It's just that I don't believe the owner would care for me going out with his good friend. It might not look too good."*

*"Nonsense! You did me a favor, and I would like to repay you. No one should have a problem with that. Tell you what, why don't you allow me to take you to lunch?"*

It had been almost a year since my husband left. Fine dining with a wealthy man in the middle of the day sure did sound good to me. After all, it was the holiday season, and it would be nice to celebrate. I agreed to go.

Placing the receiver back on the hook, I thought I must be crazy. What is everyone going to say? Somehow, between that phone call and noon the next day, I came up with the bright idea that if he liked my work so much, then just possibly he might want to hire me.

*I'm told sheep can be very naïve, yet our heavenly Father likens us to them. I can see why. Never once did I think it wasn't my office skills he was admiring.*

Nervously, I watched the clock waiting for my date with Mr. Money the next day. Following his instructions, I came out at noon thinking no one would notice Mr. Money picking me up in his customized black Mercedes with tinted windows.

He greeted me warmly, and commented on how beautiful I looked. He drove me to an exclusive French restaurant in a part of town that I wasn't aware existed. Marveling at the black gate that opened on our arrival and the attendants waiting to take the car, I remembered being overly impressed that they knew him by name, as one took his key and another one led us inside.

The host escorted Mr. Money and me to a table by the fire. As the waiter pulled out our table, we took our seats. Impressed by all the attention and service we were receiving; I opened my menu and, to my horror, realized I couldn't read one word. It was all in French!

Sensing my momentary discomfort, Mr. Money began to pronounce each entrée and describe how it was prepared. I was so impressed at his ability to speak the language that I asked him to order for me.

Conversation flowed naturally during lunch. I found him easy to talk to and managed to slip in as many credentials as possible. Finally, during dessert he asked me to share something personal with him.

*"If you could create your own utopia, what type of man would you create?"*

*"Why that's easy, Mr. Money. I would create someone like you. A man who is kind, caring, considerate, cultured, well-dressed, drives a fancy car, and has money like you."*

Sensing I had said too much, I immediately excused myself and headed off to the ladies' room and had a talk with myself. *Shari, what are you doing? I asked myself. Mr. Money is a married man. All he was doing was taking you out to lunch to say thank you! Can't you even keep that straight? Why did you have to say something so forward and needy like that!*

Ashamed that my response had revealed so much of my neediness, I eventually came out of the ladies' room. Mr. Money had settled the bill and was waiting for me in the lounge. As they brought the car around, Mr. Money kept the conversation light.

However, once inside the car he reached for my hand and, looking me directly in the eye, said,

*"I had a wonderful time and I would love to see you again."*

Immediately surges of electricity ran up and down my spine. I had heard of chemistry but never had I felt anything like this. I could hardly speak as I looked into his eyes. Finding my voice I eventually said, *"I would like that very much."* What started as a lunch date ended two years later. Mr. Money showed me how much he liked me, and I reciprocated. In the end, I became the very thing I despised: I became the other woman.

One thing is for certain. Lust and love are as different as apples and oranges. Satan, our archenemy, offers lust (immediate gratification that will leave you longing for true satisfaction in the end), and our Heavenly Father offers the real thing: love. The problem is that many times, when we are desperate and needy, we confuse the two as they both offer the potential of filling a void. However, lust rarely turns into love. Real love and trust take time to build, develop, and grow but, in the end, the results are worth the investment. I had not been willing to invest the time, nor had I been willing to wait for God to heal my broken heart. Instead I chose to be lured by Satan's lust bait. Fortunately, I serve a God who is a jealous God. He was not willing to share me with another. Thankfully, He loved me too much to leave me in that state and it wasn't long before he started sending out a rescue team to bring me back home. *Man, who wouldn't serve a God like this!*

### Confession of a Very Proud Woman

I wanted you to see me
In such a different light.
I wanted you to say
That girl, she is all right!

I wanted so badly to prove
My self-righteousness to you.
So I tried to manipulate you
With my charm and
Well-thought out views.

So perhaps you won't be surprised
At the anger I felt towards you
When you began to point out
My distorted views.
At first I felt empathy
When I perceived you misunderstood
But then again what should I expect?
We are all only human.
So I came back to plead my case.
Surely I wasn't a woman who lacked security,
Nor was I suffering from inferiority.
But you never changed your mind,
Your reasoning, or your view.
You only nodded gently and said,
"Neither Christ, nor I,
Is here to reject you."
Then I decided to write you off.
You see, I just couldn't handle
Being the one at fault.

Softly I could hear
The Holy Spirit speak to me:
"My daughter, my daughter
How I love you,
And long to set you free…"

"Free from what?" I argued.
I have it all under control.
It's not I who has a problem,
So why don't you go help John Doe!
Persistently I argued
With the Lord and with you.
But slowly it was beginning to dawn,
I was wrong and not you.
Painfully I came to the realization
That I had a problem.
And it was then I decided
To take another look
At the hill called Golgotha.
It was on that hill
My bill had been paid
Christ willingly sacrificed
His life for mine
On that blessed day.
Gently I could hear
The Holy Spirit speak to me:
I'm not that hard-nosed Father
You have painted me to be.
Nor am I the unjust judge
Who has ignored all of your pleas
On the contrary, I care so much for you

That I gave my only begotten Son
And he sacrificed his life for you!
I have so many plans in store for you
You see, before the beginning of time
I knew all about you.
Slowly I'm coming into the realization
Of the Father's love
But it's only now, only now, I can admit
I was a woman in search of the
Father's unconditional love.

# RESCUED

*"There's a way of life that looks harmless enough; look again-it leads straight to hell. Sure, those people appear to be having a good time, But all that laughter will end in heartbreak".*

Prov. 14:12 MSG

There are many problems associated with adultery. The main one is that you are involving someone else in your mess! Now it's one thing if you have never been saved, and you are just doing what your flesh feels like doing, but it is quite another thing when you are a backslider and know the way of God. My friend, let me be the first to tell you that you don't know what conviction really feels like until the love of God goes after you.

I was in sin, but I was starting to enjoy it less and less. For a season, it seemed as if everyone was talking about adultery. If I turned on the radio, inevitably the subject would turn to adultery: on the Christian and secular talk shows! Even the lyrics to some of my favorite songs seemed to betray me. I was trapped, and I soon learned that it wasn't as easy to walk away as I thought.

I began to pray in earnest, confessing my dilemma to the Lord. You see, the truth of the matter was I still loved all the stuff; the expensive gifts, the rides in his fancy cars, the times of intimacy. I loved the idea that he wasn't ashamed of me but wanted to be with me. I was bound, and I knew it. I feared the scandal in the office as a few people had already begun to make comments. But more importantly, I feared God and my soul's eternal state. In agony one day, the answer came to me:

*"Confess your faults one to another and pray for one another that you might be healed. The effectual fervent prayer of a righteous man availeth much" (James 5:16).*

Shocked, I questioned the wisdom of God. Was it true that God wanted me to tell someone that I had gotten myself trapped in sexual sins with a married man? I thought:

*"Oh Jesus I can't. There must be another way!"*

It was bad enough that I had left the church without saying a word…but to go back like this…*I just can't Lord. What would the saints say?* Unable to overcome my pride, I continued in my sins until I couldn't take it any longer. I felt like I had become involved with a demon that had the tentacles of an octopus. As soon as I would rid myself of one tentacle, it felt like nine more were surrounding me. Mustering all the confidence I could, I decided to call one of the church mothers for help one day.

*"Hello."*

*"Hello Mother. This is Shari."*

*"Shari! Girl, where have you been?"*

Very hesitantly, I opened up and shared the whole story; the betrayal, the lust, the entrapment, my inability to get free. She listened quietly as I poured out my heart. Then, with the wisdom of a mother, she began to share with me.

Love was in her voice as she encouraged me to look deep within. It took a while for me to see that I still was allowing someone else to use me. Even though I thought I was in control, I had fallen into the victim cycle again.

Without condemning me, she began to counsel me. She faithfully called me every week and encouraged me, which helped me tremendously. Slowly, I started feeling hopeful again as if there was a way out of this sinkhole I had allowed myself to become entangled in. I need to mention that she never once pressured me to come back to the church or condemned me for being so stupid; the only thing she said was that she was praying for me.

Oddly enough, that gave me a great sense of comfort. At least I was trying, and knew someone else was praying. She loved me through my mess, even though she knew I was still actively engaged in sin, and that meant more to me than I can communicate. I wasn't ready to stop yet, but I was ready to listen.

One morning, several weeks later, out of the clear, blue sky; she called me at my job with a seriousness in her voice I had never heard before. Thinking something was wrong, I asked if everything was okay, to which she replied:

*"God said you are free."*

My heart began to drop as she related her story.

*"As I was praying for you this morning, God spoke a word in my spirit. He told me to tell you he has broken the power of that spirit off of your life. You are free!"*

Now you must understand that I was not thrilled with her statement. I mean, I did want to be free, but I also wanted to continue in my acts of immorality. Mr. Money was on his way over to meet with the owner shortly, and, more than likely, drop off a key as was his custom. (Mr. Money would routinely rent a suite for our meetings then stop by the office to drop off the key for me to meet him after I got off work). I was looking forward to our meeting that night, and was unprepared for the word of the Lord to be fulfilled so soon. I had heard that when there was a true *Word from the Lord,* it would produce His desired effect! But, I would soon learn that *this* *Word* had already done that very thing.

Mr. Money came into the office later on that day, only this time he walked by me as if he hadn't seen me. Thinking that he must be late for his meeting, I easily dismissed his behavior. As the days and weeks went by, he continued to maintain a distance.

I was suddenly terminated from my job. The whole situation made no sense to me. I had been driving a sports car that was having some mechanical work done. Although I had made arrangements the day before to drop off the car and pick up a loaner, things had not worked out the way I'd planned. I had called my employer and left a message that I would not be in until the following day. Although they were extremely strict on attendance, I had not thought much about it because I had vacation time on the books, and I had just received a promotion the month before. However, as I walked into the office the next day, my boss called me in and asked why I didn't come to work the day before. When I explained the situation, he simply said:

*"I wished you had told me another reason because now I am going to have to fire you."*

I thought he was only kidding and suggested he dock me for a day's pay. However, he would not budge and, instead, told me if I wanted to apply for unemployment he would not fight me for it. I was astonished as I replied:

*"What! Are you telling me that because I missed one day from work I am fired—even though I called?"*

I was livid, and immediately sought ways to fight the case but to no avail. It was a small mom and pop shop. They could fire you at will and very little could be done.

After cleaning out my desk, I drove straight to the mother's house and poured out my complaint. Never before had I ever been fired from a job, and their reasoning was far from fair in my opinion. However, she just sat patiently and listened to my story then smiled as she told me everything would work out just fine. It took me a while before I realized the prophetic words Mother had spoken had come to pass. God had indeed broken the power of that spirit off of my life, and in His mercy completely relocated me to another job in another city. I never saw Mr. Money again!

## HUMBLED

*Once a man had two sons. The younger son said to his father, "Give me my share of the property." So the father divided his property between his two sons. Not long after that, the younger son packed up everything he owned and left for a foreign country, where he wasted all his money in wild living. He had spent everything, when a bad famine spread through that whole land. Soon he had nothing to eat. He went to work for a man in that country, and the man sent him out to take care of his pigs. He would have been glad to eat what the pigs were eating, but no one gave him a thing. Finally, he came to his senses and said, "My father's workers have plenty to eat, and here I am, starving to death! I will go to my father and say to him, 'Father, I have sinned against God in heaven and against you. I am no longer good enough to be called your son.'"*

Luke 15:11–20 (CEV)

For the next three months, I was out of work and scared. I had just rented my first apartment and rent was extremely high. At the time, I had a little red convertible that continued to break down. I was forever trying to make ends meet on a very small unemployment check. I was forced to look at my situation and face the facts. By stepping out of the ark of safety, I was in a worse state than before. I had no money, no job, no man and I had walked away from the only person who could help me in anger. Sinking in depression I began to pray: *"God, please help me!"*

And He did! The first thing he did was connect me to a prayer team. I was still not attending church on a regular basis, yet a group of ladies I had never met took it upon themselves to call me every morning at 5:00 a.m. It was a prayer chain that connected us together through a phone line. This group of ladies interceded for me until I was able to pray for myself. *There is power in prayer!*

They prayed for me until my faith was restored again. They spoke words of encouragement, hope, peace, joy, and prosperity back into my life. They prayed with me for finances and spoke of a new job with wonderful benefits that God was going to give me, and it happened! More importantly, they prayed with me until I came to myself. It was through this prayer team that one day I, like the prodigal son, returned to my Father's house (the house of the Lord) and submitted to His counsel.

Just like the prodigal son, I soon realized that bread (the word of God) was plenty, with enough to spare. No longer running from my past and accepting my present, I was willing to finally sit down and allow myself to be taught the word of God without compromise. My spiritual Father welcomed me back into the fold, and I began to hear and read the word of the Lord again.

The next seven years of my life were filled with many transformations. Following the voice of the Holy Spirit, one of the first things God led me to do was to separate myself from the familiar, kind of like Abraham when He called him to come away from his family and friends. I moved to downtown Long Beach into an apartment that I could afford. For seven years, I lived alone. I cut out dating completely. I decided that was the only way I could stop engaging in sexual immorality. It was a season of emotional repair, which required all of my attention.

The next thing God did was give me a love for his word. I became an avid reader. I tried to read every book and listen to every tape, video, or CD I could get my hands on. The more I read, listened to, and applied the word of God; the more information God supplied. I read and listened to other men and women of God continually, like a dying woman in need of a blood transfusion, until finally my life began to line up with the scriptures. I began to understand that God was not an unjust God who was out to get me for all of my failures and unholy lifestyle. On the contrary, He was a God who was full of mercy, love, and an incredible amount of patience. God opened up my understanding and increased my knowledge as He began to bless my life with love, favor and finances.

God sent all types of good people into my life. Slowly I began to change the way I dressed, the way I talked, even who I allowed to be in my inner circle. I even took my Bible to work, and many days during my lunch hour I'd simply read as I ate alone, if I didn't sneak off to the midday prayer meeting at church.

As the anointing of God increased on my life, the call of God became more and more evident. I began to speak at women's shelters, missions, prisons, and churches. Speaking in front of people seemed to come naturally for me, as the Lord would bless me to share the word of life through the anointing he had placed on me when I was a child.

For a season, it seemed as if my life was finally on the upswing. I had a great job, I was a member of a great church, I was learning how to apply God's word in my life and I was receiving tangible results. At last, everything was starting to turn around, except in one area. I still had an open door in my life that desperately needed to be closed.

Let me explain. The spirit of abuse had attached itself to me and remained since my youth. I had been hurt terribly in the church, and out of the church, by so-called Christian men. Since childhood, lewd, unsolicited, and unwelcomed comments had found their way to my ear. Now that I was in my thirties, this cycle continued. It did not seem to matter that I had gained a considerable amount of weight, and most of the time dressed down to cover up my body, I kept receiving unsolicited attention from the wrong type of men. Whether it was on my job, at the church, in my apartment complex, driving down the street, or at a grocery store, I kept attracting men with abusive spirits like a magnet. I sought God for an understanding as I prayed:

*God I don't understand. Why do men feel so comfortable saying such vulgar things to me? What is it about me that makes a man read me wrong? Why does this keep happening to me?*

Paula White once said, *"You cannot conquer what you don't challenge, and you can't challenge that which you don't face."* Although God had not given me a spirit of fear but of love, power, and a sound mind, I still was afraid to challenge the spirit of abuse. For years, I had allowed myself to be a victim. But God knew the plans he had for me. The years of tears were swiftly coming to an end as I continued to grow stronger in my understanding of what healthy boundaries were. I had the power to say no! I had the power to set boundaries and expect them not to be crossed. I was not a victim of my past but a survivor, and I had a great future in store. God loved me and wanted me to succeed in all areas of my life. Not just spiritually but in my soul (my emotions). God wanted me to experience freedom in this area too! I did not have to be ashamed of myself any longer; neither did I have to allow people to treat me any kind of way. God had already paid the price for my sins and He had adopted me into his royal family. I was a child of the King, and I was not required to let people walk over me anymore: It was time to get past my past.

As the convictions in my heart grew stronger, the day finally came when I realized it was time for me to deal with my past once and for all. No more cover up. No more excuses. No more pretending the words didn't hurt. It was time to face the pain, and eradicate it once and for all!

## CONFRONTATION

My friend once quoted me an old African proverb, *"When the student is ready the teacher will appear."* At last, I was ready to do whatever I needed to do to be free, and my heavenly Father was ready to show me. He chose to begin with Mom. One day, after much prayer, I summoned the courage to call and talk about the subject we'd both avoided for years.

My mom is one of the nicest, prettiest, and sharpest persons you could meet. She has a way of making you feel welcome and loved. When shown an error, she is quick to repent and do whatever she needs to do in order to correct it. Raised by a very strict father and emotionally unavailable mother, she had missed a lot in her early years. She had married young to get out of the house, and when her marriage failed, she spent a season in riotous living (that is she went out and did her own thing until she came to herself).

So when I called and told her what I wanted to talk about, immediately she was quiet and ready to hear. There were so many unanswered questions that I had carried around for years. Questions like:

- *Why didn't anyone talk to me and ask me what really happened?*
- *Why was I left to fend for myself?*
- *Why did they go to counseling without me?*
- *Did you really believe it was my fault?*

Naked, raw pain filled my voice as I continued to seek for answers:

*When I was a child, why didn't you see that something was wrong?*
*Why did you have to lean so much on me?*

Tears began to stream down my face as my voice finally found release:

*Why didn't you choose us (your children) instead of spending so much time with your man? Why couldn't you see how much I needed you?*

Mom responded in a voice that was filled with pain as I unleashed my anger. I wanted to stop, but I couldn't seem to turn it off. I knew she loved me, but I had so much anger stored up deep down inside that now that my voice had found release I couldn't seem to turn it off.

When I finally came up for air, I was met with the most sincere apology I could have ever heard. With a pain-filled voice she simply said:

*"I'm so sorry baby. I just didn't know how to handle it."*

From there, she began to answer my questions. No, she never thought it was my fault, nor did she ever mean to convey any accusation. She apologized if I believed she had. Then she began to explain to me what happened on the day she found the letter. She told me she had initially thrown it away without ever reading it but the Holy Spirit checked her about throwing out important papers, so she reached back into the trash and put it in her purse. When she finally read the letter, she told me that she got her gun and drove over to that pastor's house to kill him!

She then explained how she was met by his wife who pleaded and begged for his life. She encouraged her to think of us (her children) and asked her who would raise us if she were in jail. She then explained the terms of the agreement they had come to, which included counseling. She knew she needed to forgive him from her heart, so she chose to continue going to that church until she knew she had forgiven him. Then and only then, did she stop attending the church.

She never knew of the other abuses. Since I was always the strong one, it had been easy for her to lean and depend on me. She apologized over and over for the pains I had endured through her negligence, and then she began to pray for me. She asked the Lord to forgive her and heal her baby. The words of her prayer felt like liquid love being poured directly onto my broken heart.

She apologized for not sharing how special I was to her, and from that day to this she constantly conveys words of value on me over and over again telling me how much she thanks God for giving her a special daughter. Of course she feels that way about all her children and grandchildren, as well. Through trial and error she has learned how important it is to communicate these sentiments.

From that day to this, I can honestly say that I consider my mom to be one of my very best friends. *I know that she loves me and would do anything in her power to help me in any way she can.* She regularly calls and leaves messages on my machine telling me how much she loves me and how proud she is of me.

If ever a relationship was restored through the power of love and forgiveness, it is ours. I love you, Mom, and I appreciate everything you have done, and continue to do, for me. Thank you for giving me permission to share our story. May mothers all around the world learn from your example and understand the power of their words. May they have the courage to repent, if necessary, and take the time and energy required to restore their broken relationships. If God did it for us, I know He can do it for you. *Mothers, take time to tell your children how important they are, for if you don't, someone you may not want to, will.*

## THE POWER OF WORDS

*"For as he thinketh in his heart so is he"*.
Prov. 23:7

Words are so important. God spoke the world into existence through the word, and He has given us the power to do the same. That is our words, and what we allow to be spoken in our ears and received in our hearts, shape our world and our perception about others and ourselves.

Over the years, I had chosen to believe negative words about myself, and, consequently, I had developed low self-esteem. My behavior was a reflection of the way I genuinely felt about myself. Since I had not been treated with respect, I didn't demand it from others.

Did I want to be loved, valued, and treated with dignity and respect? Yes. However, since I had believed a lie from my formative years up, I was now experiencing the results. As a result, it took years for me to change the way I viewed myself. With no small effort on the part of many teachers, counselors, friends, books, videos, and tapes, my self-perception eventually began to change.

During the next few years, the Lord set the stage for me to learn how to confront unclean spirits. You might ask, what is an unclean spirit? In my case it was a very filthy, flirtatious, aggressive, bold, manipulative, suggestive spirit that was trying to coerce me to indulge in sexual acts.

One thing was certain: That foul spirit, which had harassed me since my early childhood, didn't care about me, or any long-term consequences. It just wanted to use my body to satisfy its lust and it conditioned me to attract men who would say some of the most vile, perverted things to gain my attention.

You may wonder how I could have ignored such bold suggestions. By making excuses for the other party—pretending they did not really mean what they'd just said, or by simply burying my head in the sand. That had been my MO for so long. I had learned to pretend it wasn't happening for years, and now that I was out of an abusive situation, I found it hard to believe I had gotten myself involved in another. So each time I would try that much harder to be respectable, so other men wouldn't feel comfortable disrespecting me. When I finally admitted to myself that this approach wasn't working, I started asking myself why.

Why didn't men respect me? Why did they feel so comfortable just saying anything they chose to me? What was it about me that would cause them to feel so free to tell me some of the most perverted, foul things that could ever be uttered? The answer was simple: I didn't *demand* their respect. I didn't realize that I had the power to stop it. I had become so accustomed to people saying and doing anything they wanted for so long that I didn't believe I was truly able to stop it. Thankfully, I came to realize that I was wrong—*so very wrong!*

*No one has the right to say or do anything to you unless you allow it. You have the power to say no too! If you have been abused, you must learn how stand up for yourself and draw a line in the sand. This begins by realizing your value and self-worth.*

You are worth so much. Christ died for you and sent his precious Holy Spirit to live inside of you. You are sons and daughters of the King! *Royalty demands respect.* Stop letting people talk to you any old kind of way. Stop talking to yourself in a negative manner and begin to speak words of value over your life. Your value is far greater than that which your abusers have assigned to you. You have rights! Begin by loving yourself, and then you won't allow anyone to speak to, or about, you negatively.

Once I had wholeheartedly embraced this truth—this realization, the Lord made it clear to me that there was another very important thing I had to do: finally face up to and rebuke that unclean spirit! God had given me the tools, wisdom, and strength to do it. I could no longer deny it. It was time for me to stand up to unclean spirits and say, "No more!" With the help of God, I did. I had a chance to confront and conquer my fears and, when I did, I walked away with respect and dignity.

Now I feel like a new woman, one who has been liberated and freed! *What I thought about myself had been my biggest enemy all along!* Yet, when I learned how to say what God said about me, I found it did wonders for my self-esteem.

Ladies, it doesn't matter how much weight you gain, what type of wardrobe you have (or desire to have), how you fix your hair or make up your face, real beauty starts from within. *Whatever you say about you is what you will attract.* Perhaps you are at a place where you think you can't say anything nice about you to you. I completely understand. I once was there too. God encouraged me to start reading His word and start reciting what He had to say about me. May I suggest that you do the same? Here are a few scriptures to help you build your *Word* vocabulary.

*How you made me is amazing and wonderful. I praise you for that. What you have done is wonderful. I know that very well. None of my bones was hidden from you when you made me inside my mother's body. That place was as dark as the deepest parts of the earth. When you were putting me together there, your eyes saw my body even before it was formed. You planned how many days I would live. You wrote down the number of them in your book before I had lived through even one of them. God, your thoughts about me are priceless. No one can possibly add them all up. If I could count them, they would be more than the grains of sand. If I were to fall asleep counting and then wake up, you would still be there with me.*

Psalm 139:14–18 (NIV)

*Forget the things that happened in the past. Do not keep on thinking about them. I am about to do something new. It is beginning to happen even now. Don't you see it coming? I am going to make a way for you to go through the desert. I will make streams of water in the dry and empty land.*

Isaiah 43:18–19 (NIV)

*Don't be discouraged or grow weak from fear! The LORD your God wins victory after victory and is always with you. He celebrates and sings because of you, and he will refresh your life with his love.*

Zephaniah 3:16–17 (CEV)

*But Zion said, "I don't get it. God has left me. My Master has forgotten I even exist." Can a mother forget the infant at her breast, walk away from the baby she bore? But even if mothers forget, I'd never forget you—never.*

Isaiah 49:14–16 (MSG)

*"Fear not, for I am with you; Be not dismayed, for I am your God. I will strengthen you, Yes, I will help you, I will uphold you with My righteous right hand".*

Isa. 41:10 NKJV

God's Word has so much to say about you and how much value God has placed on you. He loves you and longs for you to see how beautiful you really are!

# D-DAY!

At last, the time came for me to confront my Dad. It had been almost twenty years since I'd talked to him. I had been so hurt that my father had not bothered to come to my wedding, yet managed to come to the hospital to see his firstborn grand-daughter months later, that I made myself a promise that I would never reach out to him again. If he wanted to see me, from now on, he would have to make the effort. Little did I know God had another plan!

Some years later, the Holy Spirit unlocked the final door, as he revealed the condition of my heart through a counseling session I had with my new pastor. Out of the blue, my pastor asked me a question that was completely unrelated to the issue we were discussing, yet it would serve as the key to unlock the door to the root of my problem. The question was simply this: "*When was the last time you spoke to your dad?*" Without giving it a second, thought I instantly replied:

"*I made a vow that I was never going to speak to my father again!*"

I immediately placed my hands over my mouth, but it was too late. The condition of my heart had been exposed. It was impossible for him, or me, to ignore the venom that had just spewed out of my mouth. Undeniably, I was filled with anger and unforgiveness. And, to make matters worse, I didn't even know it until that moment! Lovingly, but very firmly, he looked me dead in the eyes and said:

*"You need to find your father and ask him to forgive you."*

I responded: *"What? Ask him to forgive me?"* I continued, hardly able to believe what I was hearing. *"Why on earth would I want to do that? The last time I checked, he was the one who left me!"*

Ignoring my outrage, he proceeded: *"And you need to forgive him."*

I was furious! Before I knew it, tears began to flood my eyes. Neither he, nor God, could possibly be serious! After all of these years, the Lord used my pastor to uncover a root of bitterness I didn't even know I had. Unbelievable! True to form, my response was an immediate. *"No way! I'm not going to do it!"*

Unmoved by my emotions, the wisdom of God continued to pour out of my pastor's mouth:

*"Then and only then will you break this generational curse, and then your blessings will begin to spring forth."*

With those final words he began to pray:

*"Father, bless Sis Shari to find and forgive her dad…"*

Outraged, I thought about everything I had been through and wondered what forgiving my father had to do with my future. What about all the hurt and rejection his leaving had caused me? As far as I was concerned, my father didn't have a clue, and judging by his lack of actions, he didn't even care!

My pastor obviously didn't understand the dynamics involved. My dad had remarried years ago and had another family. He rarely called or checked on us before he remarried. Once he remarried, it seemed like he didn't have time for his children anymore. Why would he want to be bothered with me now? Right then and there, my stubborn will reared its ugly head, as I began to vent my frustrations to the Lord:

*"I don't want to do it Lord. I don't want to, and I won't!"*

At the time, I couldn't see past my hurt and pain. I couldn't bear the thought of reaching out for love, his love, only to be rejected again. As I continued to vent my frustrations to the Lord, my emotions eventually began to subside. Still trying to persuade the Lord, I continue to argue my case: *Lord, I have already made it this far without his help. What is the point of looking back now?*

Little did I know that God already had a plan for us to meet in motion. Six months earlier, as I was enjoying a birthday breakfast with one of my friends, one of the servers approached the table and, after greeting my friend, looked at me and said: *"You look just like my stepdaughter."*

I was reviewing some paperwork, but I looked up to see who she was talking about when I heard her comment. To my surprise, I found myself staring into the face of my stepmom when I did. So many emotions flooded my mind as I received her warm embrace. I barely had a chance to recover, before she began to chasten me for not coming by to see my dad:

*"Shari, you know you guys really need to come by and see your dad. It's a shame how none of you kids come by and see him."*

I suppose bitterness, anger, and hurt couldn't have chosen a better moment to raise its ugly head. How could she look me in my face and tell me what I needed to do? Something on the inside of me broke. I was so tired of stuffing my emotions as I put on a happy face for the world to see. I thought to myself, *since when do children arrive on earth to take care of their parents?* All of my life, I grew up trying to please everyone, especially my parents. I suddenly snapped, and all I could hear were words of guilt and condemnation ringing in my head. My look must have portrayed what I felt, because my friend, who also was a licensed counselor, grabbed my hand and asked me if I was okay the moment my stepmom walked away.

"*No, I'm not! I'm not okay!*" I responded.

Then, I practically screamed as I unleashed my fury:

"*What about the things they are supposed to do? The last time I checked, I was the child. She was the one who took my daddy away some twenty years ago and left me and my family to live in a rat and roach infested house with little food and money to buy clothes. She knew he had four kids before she married him. Why hadn't she encouraged him to stop by and see his kids or require him to send money so we could have some of the things we needed? Did she ever think we might want some new school clothes instead of hand-me-downs? What about Christmas presents? Just one time in these last twenty years, did they even think to pick up the phone and call us? Not only did I not know the number, I didn't even know where they lived!*"

My stepmom had no idea of the displaced anger that raged in my soul. Returning to the table, she gave me their number and urged me to call my dad. Hardening my heart, I told her today was my birthday and if he wanted to show me how much he loved me, then she could have him pick up the phone and call me. Coming to his defense, she immediately responded:

"*Shari, you know that he isn't physically able to pick up the phone and call.*"

Unmoved by her plea, I responded in anger, "*Then why don't you do it for him!*"

The call never came, but for some reason I didn't throw the number away. Now, weeks after the meeting with my pastor, I had a decision to make.

Did I want to break this victim cycle, or did I want to hang on to unforgiveness?

As I reasoned within myself, I began to think:

*"If releasing my dad would actually break this cycle I continually find myself in, wouldn't it be worth it?"*

Over the past year, the Lord had used my pastor to help me overcome quite a few problems. Submitting to his counsel and trusting in God's sovereignty had set me free from so much emotional bondage. Why should this be any different? As I begin to ponder my dilemma, my mind went back to the day I first met my new pastor. As he walked into the room, the Lord spoke to my heart and told me he held the answer to a lot of my problems. At that moment, I knew I had the answer. Now all I had to do was act on the information.

After letting out a big sigh, I decided to call. This would be my first time to call my father in almost twenty years. I picked up the receiver and finally found the courage to dial. My heart was racing as I began to wonder what to say. The telephone rang several times, but to no avail. I began to panic.

*Had my stepmom given me the right number? Did I write it down wrong?*

I was so focused on the idea of my dad answering the telephone that I was surprised by the electronic voice from an answering machine stating:

*"No one is available to take your call right now. Please leave a message after the tone."*

I started talking, hoping my dad would answer:

*"Hello, this is Shari. Is anybody home? I'm trying to reach my dad. If anyone is there can you please pick up?"*

After waiting a few seconds I decided to leave a message.

*"Okay...I guess no one is home. Can someone please give me a call back?"*

Leaving my telephone number, I quickly hung up the telephone wondering if anyone would ever call me back. It would take several more calls before my stepmom called me back. She had been caring for my Dad for over twenty years, as a drunk driver hit him when he was on his way home from work. The accident had left him paralyzed—initially from his neck down. He regained some movement in his upper body but was never been able to walk again. My stepmom had faithfully cared for him. Since he was confined to a wheelchair, my stepmom had become was very protective of him. She did not want me to get his hopes up by promising to visit then not showing up. It took quite a bit of convincing before she agreed to let me talk to my dad.

Finally, after many calls, and a very serious conversation with my stepmom, the miracle happened. I arrived home from work one day and hit the button on my answering service to retrieve my messages, when I nearly fainted, as I heard this broken voice, trying to hold back tears, say:

*"Hello Shari. This is your Dad…"*

I couldn't believe it. My father's voice was actually on my answering service. He sounded like a broken man. Leaving the most beautiful message on my service, he conveyed his sentiments and asked me to return his call at my convenience. I didn't quite know what to do. I had to sit down as I replayed the message over and over again. I called my friend and allowed her to listen to the message. With her encouragement, I summoned up the courage to call.

This time my stepmom answered and put him on the phone. What a wonderful conversation we had. We set up a date to meet. When I hung up, I was excited. After all this time, I was actually going to see my dad. I couldn't wait to call my sister and brother and tell them the good news. I had a meeting to see Dad!

## REUNITED

The plan had been made, and a surge of emotions over-whelmed me as I was preparing to meet dad:

*Oh God, help me! I can't believe it's already after five o'clock. I should have left the office an hour ago. There is no way I'm going to make it by six o'clock now. Maybe I should just call and reschedule. After all, what difference is one more day going to make anyway? Although, if I hurry just maybe I can still make it. Let's see, where did I place those directions again?*

One hour later I sat down in a coffee shop. Of all nights, why did traffic have to be so bad? Why didn't I see the off ramp? How could I get so lost? I became uneasy. Everything inside of me said, "Turn around and forget the whole thing."

Listening to my inner turmoil I thought:

*After all what's the point in trying to make it now? You blew it, so you might as well turn around. You are already late anyway. How is that going to look? Your first meeting in almost twenty years and you show up late. Just call and cancel.*

These thoughts and more ran through my mind as I slowly drank my coffee. But then I heard another voice:

*Shari, get a hold of yourself! Pull yourself together, and snap out of this. So much is riding on your obedience. I'm going to be right there with you. Everything is going to be okay. Let's go!*

I gathered my things, got back into my car, and back on the road. At last I found the house. I arrived almost two hours late. Feeling unsettled and distressed, I thought:

*Oh God, I blew it. Surely he would not want to see me now.*

As I sat sulking in the car, debating whether to get out or simply drive away, my eyes landed on the house. To my surprise there he was, sitting in a wheelchair in the middle of the picture frame window waiting for me. *I couldn't believe it! My father was actually waiting for me!*

I took a quick look in the mirror, nervous and excited at the same time. At last, I was going to be reunited with my dad! I walked up to the door and took a deep breath before I knocked. My stepmother greeted me warmly as I walked in. There he was. With arms wide open, he burst into tears while repeatedly saying, "*Thank you Lord,*" over and over again. To hear him pray so earnestly broke the ice around my heart. He said he had one request before he died: to be reunited with his children. Wow!

I sat down in the living room in amazement. Floods of questions began to pour through my mind. *If you wanted to be reconnected, why didn't you call or come by? Why weren't you there for us all of those years?*

As if he knew what I was thinking, without any prompting from me, Daddy began to apologize for all the years he missed. As the tears flowed, he kept asking me to forgive him unashamedly. Imagine that! *My father was actually apologizing to me!*

For a second, it seemed like all the pain and anger I had carried around for years began to fade, as I looked into my daddy's eyes. I wanted to forgive him. I wanted to let it go, but

I just couldn't—not yet. Too much time had passed, and even though I knew he was sincere, I just wasn't there yet.

My stepmother had stepped out of the room to give us some privacy but eventually returned and began to talk about their lives together. What had the last twenty-four years been like since Daddy had that accident?

She spoke of their two sons and the phone ministry Daddy had developed. Looking around at their furnishings, my eyes fell on the bookshelf. I realized that we had similar taste in books. Daddy gladly allowed me to borrow a few books as I commented to my stepmother on what a beautiful home she had made for my dad. Not many women would have stuck by their man like she had. I was eternally grateful. Daddy looked great!

Then, all too soon, the visit was over. My dad had been sitting up for quite a while and I could see that he needed to rest. As I made my way to the door, I promised to come back with my other siblings. His face was aglow as I mentioned bringing my brother and sisters. Any misgivings I might have had about his sincerity were quickly erased.

*"Do you really think they would want to come by and see me?"*

My heart broke. The separation Daddy had endured had taken its course. Quickly, I responded:

*"Of course they will, Daddy! Of course!"*

The peace that came over his face was priceless. I knew my brother and sisters would eventually come around, especially after I shared with them what had just occurred. That evening I drove home in a daze. I had just been reconnected to my dad and my feelings were all over the place.

Over the next few weeks, we made arrangements for all four of us to go together and visit Daddy. *What a celebration of reconcil-*

*iation!* Daddy utilized the time he had with each one of us quite well. One by one, he called each one of us into the room and made his peace with God and us. He apologized to each of us individually for not being there and begged our forgiveness.

How I would love to tell you I took advantage of our time together, but I didn't. I can't explain it, but something still didn't feel right. I knew that he was sincere and all, but it takes time to build trust. I guess for me too much had happened for me to let it go just yet.

Sitting in a funeral service a few weeks later, all of the sudden I had a strange feeling as if something was terribly wrong. I took out my cell phone and noticed my sister had called. When I called her back, she was with Daddy. He had been taken to the emergency room. He was having some chest pains and went to get it checked out. The hospital wasn't too far from the church. I decided to drive to the hospital and check the situation out for myself.

Anxiety filled my thoughts as I walked into Daddy's room. My sister was getting ready to give him something to drink with his lunch. Looking up at me, he immediately gave me his million-dollar smile. The he looked at my sister and said, *"Here comes trouble!"*

Daddy always had a way of making me laugh. Even though he was lying in a hospital bed waiting for the results of his test, today would prove to be no different. Before I could make a smart reply, daddy began to gasp for air. The nurse came in the room and escorted everyone out immediately as one of the medical staff members called code blue.

I was scared, and I called my pastor. Fortunately my pastor's wife answered the phone. Ignoring formality I went straight to the point: *"Hello First Lady, this is Shari. I'm at the hospital with my dad, and they just called code blue. Please pray!"*

First Lady heard the fear in my voice and immediately went into prayer. I don't think I have ever felt my heart race with such intensity before. After she calmed me down, she assured me she would give Pastor the message and they would continue to pray. I felt better already.

I waited nervously in the lobby with my sister as we both prayed Daddy would be okay. Once we were assured Daddy was okay, I left my number, requesting a call if there were any changes in his condition. Deep down inside, I had a feeling that everything was not really okay, but at the time I was unable to deal with it. I had only been reunited with my dad for a few months and I was not ready to face the possibility of losing him just yet. It was just a few chest pains. How bad could it be?

A few days later, the call came. Daddy was scheduled for surgery. He had been transported to another hospital where they immediately recognized the gravity of his situation. Heart surgery had been ordered. I dropped everything and raced to the hospital.

Isn't it funny how you can prioritize things when it's a matter of life and death? All of a sudden nothing I was doing, or had scheduled, was important. Driving down the freeway like a mad woman, I had only one thought in my head. *Daddy, please don't go!*

How foolish had I been to hold on to my pride. Even when he reached out and asked me to forgive him, I never asked him to forgive me. I had been so self-righteous in holding onto my anger and grief that I failed to take advantage of the opportunity God afforded us both. What about the years I had ignored him? What about the pleas from those who knew him that begged me to release my anger and go to see him? What about the years I wasted because I wanted so much to prove my point? What difference did it make now?

That's when it hit me. All the years I had lost blaming the world for my plight, as I continuously looked for love in all the wrong places: genuine love had been waiting for me all along. All I had to do was swallow my pride and pick up the phone!

*Oh my God what have I done? I have robbed each of us of the opportunity to get to know each other for so many years.* How long had he sat in that chair unable to walk, or laid in bed unable to move, praying to God for his family and one more chance to make it right. I could have helped to give him relief. Instead, I chose to act as if he no longer existed.

Sitting in that car, I was paralyzed with fear. I wanted to go back to the beginning. I wanted to experience being his little girl again. I wanted him to protect me. I wanted him to love me. I wanted him to keep me safe from all those evil men. If I could have my way, I wished we could just start all over again. I began to cry. *"Oh God please don't take my dad! I just found him. Please don't take him home yet!"*

There were so many things I needed to say. I needed to ask him to forgive me for holding on to anger and unforgiveness for so many years. I wanted him to forgive me for acting as if I had never done anything wrong. The truth of the matter was I had the power to release him years ago. Instead, I chose to withhold my love and judge him. The choices I'd made only ended up hurting me in the end. I wanted another chance to tell him what I truly wanted to say:

*"Oh Daddy, there were so many things I just didn't know. I thought you missed my wedding because you didn't care. I didn't know you missed*

*my wedding because there were no provisions for wheelchairs. All this time I didn't know you couldn't hold a phone. I held you accountable for things you could not even do. Oh Daddy, please forgive me…"*

Sitting in the hospital that Saturday, I waited in the lobby with the family. When the doctors finally came out, the news was not good. They had given him a triple bypass and one lung had collapsed. It was so hard to see my dad in that condition. He was hooked up to several machines and tubes were going everywhere. In order for him to receive oxygen, the doctors had to cut a hole in his throat, preventing him from speaking ever again.

For a while I tried to visit, but I hated seeing my dad in that condition. Daddy was a proud man, and in my heart I do not believe he wanted us to see him incapacitated. After a while, I became guilt-ridden and simply stopped visiting him.

God blessed me with a wonderful friend who encouraged me to go and visit my dad. She would often drive me to the hospital (some sixty miles away) and sit and talk with him when I couldn't. What amazed me was, even though he could not talk, he never failed to flash that beautiful smile whenever we entered into his room. *It was as if he was trying to be strong for us!*

I couldn't take it. It took so little to make him smile. I realized too late that he really did love us and would have enjoyed just having us around. It took me looking at my father on his deathbed to realize all the grudges I had been holding all these years were against the wrong person.

It wasn't my Daddy's fault that I had suffered abuse. Neither was it my mother's fault. It was the enemy, Satan the devil, who was out to kill, steal, and destroy my life though the sick ideas he planted into the minds of my predators. They chose to carry out Satan's plan, and I chose to respond with self-pity, denial, anger, and bitterness. In the end it cost me dearly. *My friend, if there is anyone in your life you are holding negative feelings against please choose to process them, release them, and let them go!*

Ultimately only you have the power to decide how you will respond. Choose to forgive, and, if possible, set healthy boundaries for yourself. Enjoy healthy relationships with those you love. Burying your head in the sand and wishing it would all go away is not the answer. You have to deal with it. You have the power to change your life. You cannot go back, but you can go forward. Cherish the relationships God has blessed you to have and leave vengeance to the Lord. He will repay.

## DADDY DON'T GO!

*Two years later my father died.* Sitting in the funeral home, I looked at my dad. My stepmom had dressed him in his favorite colors. He looked extremely handsome, even in death. Trying to take it all in, I could do nothing but sit.

The last few days had gone by in a blur. I had received the news of his death while at work. Normally, I don't like to check my messages at work but for some reason, during my break, I did. One number stood out above all others. I decided to call. It was my regional missionary. She was my half-brother's mother-in-law.

Her voice sounded grave. Endeavoring to be tactful, she asked me if I had heard the news. Instantly I knew. She said that she wasn't sure but she believed my dad had just passed, and suggested I call my sister-in-law to verify the information. I called her right away but there was no answer.

I walked into my supervisor's office and told her I believed my dad had died. I'm sure that I looked as if I had seen a ghost because she instantly came to my desk and told me to leave. She said she would take care of everything. When I arrived at my car, I called my mom. I couldn't keep my hands from shaking.

At the sound of my voice, she asked me what was wrong. I told her Daddy just died and asked her if she would call my brother and sisters to let them know. It was rush-hour traffic, and it would take me at least an hour to get to the hospital. As the tears began to flow, I pulled over to the side of the road and broke down. My sister-in-law called back and confirmed the news. Daddy had indeed died.

I don't know why, but for some reason I felt the need to stop and get some ice cream. Daddy and I had both enjoyed eating black walnut ice cream, and for some reason that memory came back to my mind. I stopped at a Baskin-Robbins and ordered a kiddy scoop.

I decided to go home. When I arrived at my house, I turned on a movie and just sat there eating ice cream. My sisters and brother had been calling along with a few other friends. The news traveled quickly, but I was unable to answer any phone calls, at least not yet. I just sat there eating ice cream and watching the tube. Finally, my sister and brother came over to my house and insisted that I go with them to see my stepmom.

Once again, looking for somebody to blame, anger filled my heart as I wondered why my stepmom didn't call. Why didn't she tell us my father had taken a turn for the worse and been moved to the ICU? Why did I have to hear it from my regional missionary instead of her? Wasn't it enough that she had him for all of these years? Couldn't she have shared him in death?

I learned that once again my anger had been displaced. She explained that she had just left the hospital and he was doing just fine. He had mouthed three words to her early that week and she believed he had said, "*Let me go.*" She was just as shocked as we were that he'd died. In my heart, I knew she was telling the truth.

My brother insisted that all of the children go out. We sat at Norm's until after midnight swapping stories and fond memories we had of Daddy. The funeral was held the following Saturday. Dressed in black, I sat with the family trying to disconnect my mind from the events that were unfolding before my eyes.

*Daddy was dead.* Just like that. How my heart ached to have him back. I was glad he was no longer in pain, yet I still felt so cheated. I wanted to enjoy his life with him. I wanted to hear his voice and see his smile one more time. I did not want to pretend everything was okay. It was not. My daddy was dead and there was nothing I could do about it.

As the service progressed, we (the children) were given an opportunity to express our sentiments. One by one, we each took the podium and looked over the audience of friends and family who had taken out time to share in our grief. When my turn came I rose hesitantly. All I wanted to do was break down and cry, but as I looked at the faces of all the beautiful people my family and I had been blessed to know, I realized it was indeed a celebration. Daddy was no longer in pain, and the best part was he had a chance to reconcile with God and his family (including my mom who came to the hospital to extend her forgiveness to him as well) before he died.

With one last poem, I celebrated my father's life, and I am eternally grateful God gave us the chance to reconcile before he died. My daddy is in heaven now: walking, talking, and waiting for all of us to get there. For the short period of time that we shared, I realized my daddy possessed the traits of a sensitive, caring, wonderful, God-fearing man who was blessed with good looks, a sharp mind, and a wonderful personality. As we exchanged books, laughter, and love Daddy etched an eternal place in my heart. I only wish I had taken advantage of all the chances I had to get to know him a long time ago.

## LIFE AFTER DAD

After the death of my dad, I realized that I still had some serious problems that I needed to deal with. For one thing, I was seriously overweight, and had been for years. I had being fighting the battle of the bulge, yet I had been seriously losing the war. Instead of getting smaller, I was getting bigger. I had become addicted to fast food and at one point, I topped the scales weighting 338 pounds. Did I mention that I am only five-foot-two?

While it was true that I was concerned about my weight, I had not been willing to change my diet or seriously consider an exercise program. Walking for long extended times was a challenge for me. My back used to hurt, and occasionally my knees, if I tried to do squats. However, I was greatly concerned that if I continued to do nothing, I would start having some serious health problems. I knew the origin of my pain came from the sexual and emotional abuse I suffered in my childhood, but I didn't have a clue as to how to resolve it. What I needed was a plan on how to replace my faulty thinking and negative behaviors. So, I did what Jehoshaphat did. I cried out to God in desperation:

*Oh Lord, please help me. I don't know what to do about my weight anymore.*
*"Be obedient."*
*What? Be obedient?*
*"Learn to submit and obey."*

Instantly, I knew what the Holy Spirit was speaking about. It was the first of the year and our church was to begin a twenty-one-day consecration. Our pastor had given instructions that we were to fast every day until 3:00 p.m. except Sunday. We could eat after the service on Sunday.

I realized the fast was to start the next day. I had considered fasting a few days maybe, but certainly not twenty-one whole days! That seemed impossible for someone who planned her day thinking about where I was going to eat. *"Lord are you saying for the next twenty-one days you want me to go without food until 3:00 p.m.? Lord, do you remember that I am the one who likes to eat, even when I'm not hungry?"* The whole notion seemed ludacris to me. I was a food junkie. In fact, I had started eating at this one restaurant so regularly that I knew all the morning crew by name including the manager and busboy! To give up breakfast and lunch for twenty-one days seemed almost laughable. However, I was desperate enough to give it a try.

*Father, you said all things are possible to those that believe. I have never fasted for twenty-one days straight, but with your help I believe I can do this. So Holy Spirit, as an act of my will, I choose to surrender my appetite to you right now. May my desire to please you be greater than my desire to satisfy my stomach.*

Reading my Bible later on that day, this passage of scripture really spoke to my heart:

*"Tomorrow, march out against them. Take your positions; then stand still and watch the LORD's victory. Do not be afraid or discouraged. Go out against them tomorrow, for the LORD is with you!" (2 Chron. 20:15 NLT).*

## LET THE FAST BEGIN

Lord, please show me the root
I don't understand
Why I keep running to food instead of you?
It never leaves me
satisfied for long,
And in the end, I only feel worse.

Oh God, Please Help Me!
I am tired of being out of control
I want my power back
I want my body back
I want to be the person
You created me to be...

### *Fasting Journal*

**Day One:** Well, the fast starts today. I am a little nervous and apprehensive that I won't be able to go the distance. We are supposed to fast every day for the next twenty-one days until 3:00 p.m. In the interim, we are to pray and read three chapters from our Bible every day. *Wow Lord, how am I ever going to do this? I haven't given up food in a long time and even though it's only till three, I don't know whether or not I can do this. Please help me Lord. I want to be obedient and go the distance but I don't know if I can.* I didn't work out today, but I did fast until 3:00 p.m. I'm feeling pretty proud of myself. Thank you, Lord! I didn't think I could do it, but with your help, I did.

**Day Two:** I'm hungry, but if I can just make it until after service I will be good. Thankfully pastor said we could eat right after service. I am going to the 8:00 a.m. service instead of the 11:30 service today so I can eat sooner. Thank God! No exercise for me today. It's Sunday, and I have a full day. Maybe I will try to do something on Monday. I'm just happy I have made it through the fast for two days in a row!

**Day Three:** Tomorrow is my birthday and I have two invitations for breakfast and three invitations for dinner. Maybe I can be excused from fasting tomorrow. After all, it is my birthday and I haven't broken the fast yet. This is my third day fasting. Kudos to me! Not much exercise though.

**Day Four:** Wow Lord, I can't believe I'm another year older. Even though I'm tired, I'm kind of looking forward to prayer and working out today. I can always come back home and go back to sleep before I start celebrating my birthday. After prayer, I was able to work out for over an hour today with no problem. Yay team! I even added five pound weights to my workout and did some floor crunches. My stomach is a little sore, but I feel good. I have decided not to break my fast today.

**Day Six:** Today is the sixth day of my fast. God is helping me. There is no way I could do this without Him and I'm working out too! I didn't make it to the 5:00 a.m. prayer, but I did make it to the 6:00 a.m. prayer. A few of the sisters from the first session were still hanging around and told me they are starting to see a difference; they actually said they saw my hips coming down. Now, that was a big compliment! I don't really see anything, but

I am really focused on being obedient right now. I truly want to successfully complete this fast, but it is getting harder each day. I worked out to a new CD today. It was so good that I actually forgot about my hunger pains. I kept playing this one track over and over again, as I allowed the words to minister to my soul. The chorus was: I can see a new day dawning. I can see breakthrough coming. Joy is coming. Breakthrough…breakthrough! I was so caught up in the prophetic worship that I began to sing and praise while I worked out on the elliptical machine. Before I knew it, the hour was over! I felt so good that I decided to do a few floor exercises and lift a few weights, as well.

**Day Seven:** This is the seventh day of the fast and I am officially sick of fasting! I am tired and I want to eat breakfast, lie in bed, and watch movies. It's been a really long week and I feel like I deserve a break. I am tired and I don't want to get up and go to church! Yet in my heart, I know this is the only way I am going to be able to stay on my fast today. If I stay home, I am going to eat for sure. Besides, the pastor has requested that we go to one of the Bible studies. If I am going to obey leadership, I need to get up. It's already after eight and Bible study starts at nine. OMG!

The message was really good. I actually bought the CD. It helped me so much that later, when I went to prayer, I was able to confide to one of the elders my feelings. He prayed for me, anointed me with oil, and asked the Holy Spirit to grace me to not quit. I'm starting to realize this is not about me, or how I feel about fasting, but it's about my obedience. Okay Lord, I choose to obey the directive for this house and keep on fasting.

**Day Eight:** It's Sunday morning and I have decided to try on a skirt that I have not been able to button. It's still tight, but I can get it on and if I hold my stomach in, I can button it up. Maybe in another month I will be able to wear it comfortably. For some reason, I received quite a few compliments today. I still don't see much of anything, but I'm encouraged to stay the course.

After the fast today, I pressed the panic button. In hindsight, I wonder how receiving those compliments affected me. I stopped at a fast food chain and I ate a cheeseburger with fried zucchini and even had a soda. Three hours later I stopped again and had a cookie and a cup of coffee. Then, after evening service I had a late-night snack: a ham and cheese sandwich with mayonnaise and a granola bar. Emotional eating…what's that all about?

**Day Nine:** I took the day off to get some much needed rest. I learned a hard lesson yesterday. When I am tired and emotionally drained, I need to rest, not eat. Thankfully, yesterday was a free day and today I am choosing to keep on fasting.

**Day Ten:** I went back to 5:00 a.m. prayer this morning. The Lord woke me up at 4:00 a.m. To be honest, I thought I would sleep through this morning on account of going to bed so late, but God, who is always faithful, woke me up in time and I made it to prayer on time. Working out was really hard today, but after forty minutes, I started to feel better and finished my hour plus added floor exercise and weights today. Wow Jesus, I can't believe I'm still holding on to the fast!

**Day Thirteen:** Received a great revelation from the Holy Spirit regarding our lack of faith and power in the body of Christ. The passage the Lord showed me was about a father who brought his son to the disciples to be healed. He wanted them to cast a demon out of His son but they could not. In fact, the scripture says, "I brought him to your disciples, but they could not heal him" (Matt. 17:16 NIV).

The Lord then showed me how the world is coming to the church for answers. How they are looking to us to have the power to heal the sick, cast out devils, preach the gospel (the good news) and when we don't, they are left to go back into the world to find solutions. We, as the body of Christ, are supposed to be anointed with the Holy Ghost and power so that we can do good, and heal all that are oppressed of the devil like Jesus did (see Acts 10:38). But we can't do this as long as we allow "sin to reign in our body" and give up our authority. We can rise up, however, and reclaim our authority over the all the power of the enemy, but first, we must take control over ourselves. Romans 6:12 says, "Let not sin therefore reign in your mortal body, that ye should obey it in the lusts thereof."

**Day Fifteen:** Today, as I was working out, a spirit of repentance fell on me. I began to weep as I repented to God for abusing my body. I saw the truth of what I have done. I have abused another man's property. My body belongs to the Lord, and I do not have the right to abuse it by eating whatever I want, whenever I want. I am to take care of the Lord's property. I can no longer refuse to exercise just because I don't feel like it. This is the revelation I received after reading the scripture found in 1 Corinthians 6:19–21 (WE):

*Do you not know that your body is the house of the Holy Spirit who lives in you? God gave the Holy Spirit to you. Remember, you do not belong to yourself. But you were bought and paid for. So then, bring glory to God with your bodies.*

I truly repented before the Lord today and asked him to restore every vital organ to its original working condition. I was really grieved by my arrogance. What right do I have to treat something God gave me so carelessly?

**Day Sixteen:** I woke up with breakfast on my mind. I'm tired of fasting. I want to eat. The Lord provided a distraction for me this morning and it took my mind off food. Later on, I went to noonday prayer and finished my errands. Actually, I did not eat till almost 6:00 p.m. Wow! God is so good to me. I didn't think I could take another day of fasting, and today I went three hours longer than what was required. Thanks Lord!

**Day Seventeen:** This is the seventeenth day of the fast! I made it to 6:00 a.m. prayer this morning then preceded immediately to the gym for my morning workout. It was hard, because it's been a few days and my body is protesting. I just have to remind myself that my body doesn't get a vote, and it must comply. I completed a little over an hour of cardio and weights (I added more weights to the routine this morning). I started feeling better about forty minutes into the workout. Note to self: Do some movement on the days you are not going to the gym, or it will be too hard to get back into the routine once you come back.

**Day Nineteen:** I received a wonderful vision today. I saw a horse trainer taking his horse out and walking him around the track. The horse was being led by his trainer with a rope, and the beautiful thing was the horse was not resisting. I heard the Lord say I am his racehorse and he wants to train me. Then the Lord showed me how I had been running restless and wild for a season, but now that I was willing to become submissive to his will, He was able to lead me around the track and eventually He was going to run me. Wow! I honestly can't see myself "running" anywhere right now, but if that's what He said, I stand in agreement. I declare, "Lord, I am willing to become a racehorse for you." *"And blessed is she that believed: for there shall be a performance of those things which were told her from the Lord"* (Luke 1:45 KJV).

**Day Twenty-One:** I am a few hours away from finishing my first twenty-one-day fast. I can't believe it. OMG! With the help of the Holy Ghost I made it through! Oh Lord, you are awesome! Thank you for helping me complete my first twenty-one-day fast.

### *Vision of the Chopping Board*

After the fast, my church held a prayer breakfast to celebrate the end of the fast. While attending the prayer breakfast, I saw a vision. I saw a big kitchen and in the middle of the kitchen, I saw a big island that had a cutting board with a piece of meat lying on top.

As I looked closer, I saw that a drawer had been opened and a sharp knife had been selected. I then heard in my spirit the Lord say, He is the master chef and every instrument in the kitchen belongs to Him. He then revealed to me that He was about to use a certain person to "cut" on me, and that I would be fine as long as I remembered that "the tool" was in His hand.

As soon as I had that vision, one of the sisters sitting at the table with me, placed her hand on my forehead and with tears streaming down her face began to pray earnestly for me. Somehow, I just knew that I had been anointed for my burial (that is, my flesh was getting ready to go through a death process).

Turns out I was right, as over the next nine months, God began to teach me how to identify and correct unhealthy thoughts and behaviors rooted in my soul. I was soon to learn that while I was focusing on losing body fat, God was focusing on me losing the excess emotional baggage (i.e. my faulty logic, irrational beliefs, thought processes, and behaviors) that were weighing my soul down.

## IDENTIFYING STRONGHOLDS

*"Search me, O God, and know my heart: try me, and know my thoughts: And see if there be any wicked way in me, and lead me in the way everlasting".*

Ps. 139:23–24

I once heard an old African proverb that states when the student is ready, the teacher will appear. I was ready to learn and the Holy Spirit was ready to teach me how to identify and cast down strongholds that I had erected in my soul; my mind, my will and emotions. God began the process of showing me what strongholds were by drawing my attention to a tree whose roots were so big that they were actually coming out of the ground! I had been looking at the tree and wondering how long ago it was planted when I heard a still quite voice say, "My love is strong enough to uproot anything that has been planted in your life."

Wow! I knew the enemy had planted some bad seeds in me that had developed some strong roots. My fruit was now being manifested by all the lies and deceptions I had believed from childhood up. Most of them were planted when I was a small child. Yet, now as an adult, it was my job to measure my thought life against the word of God, and pull down any thoughts that were not in line with His Word.

The problem was I *knew* the Word but, I didn't know how to successfully apply the Word on a practical level in my life.

The same truth applied to me regarding strongholds. I could quote the well-known passage found in 2 Corinthians 10:5 that spoke about "casting down imaginations and every high thing that exalted itself against the knowledge of God," but since I didn't even know what a stronghold was, I certainly didn't know how to cast it down!

Thankfully, my Father knew that I didn't know either. He also knew I couldn't wage war successfully if I didn't learn how to use the armor He had left, which led to Him giving me my next set of instructions on how to identify strongholds.

In order for me to be healed, I had to allow the Lord to examine my soul and submit to His process. The first stronghold He identified was fear. I decided to get a dictionary and look up the word. According to the Merriam-Webster Dictionary, to be full of fear means to be full of terror, dread, horror, fright, panic, alarm, trepidation, or apprehension. Was it true that fear was at the root of my obesity?

The more I thought about it, the more I realized the Holy Spirit had indeed unveiled the root of my problem: fear! You see, at an early age, I learned how to stuff my emotions. I had learned to be quiet and do what I was told. I learned how to submit to molestation. I was too afraid to tell anyone what was going on, and I carried that childhood pain inside for years.

I can still remember the day when I made the decision to overeat. A male friend of the family was checking me out and told me that I was a "fox." To me, that meant more men were going to be checking me out and I didn't want that to happen. So, I made the decision to become fat. I thought this would make me less attractive.

Sadly, I bought the lie that if I gained weight and kept it on, men wouldn't find me attractive and try to come on to me. At first, it was just a little weight gain. No more than ten to twenty pounds above the normal weight for my height.

Then, I moved up to a size twelve in my late teens and early twenties. After marriage, I went to a fourteen, then an eighteen. I ultimately ended up in a size twenty-four after the divorce. Hiding behind weight didn't work then and it wasn't working now.

## PRIDE AND UNFORGIVENESS

One day at the 8:00 a.m. church service, God placed His finger on another area in my life where I had unhealed hurts that I had covered up with unforgiveness and pride. This truth was revealed to me while I was sitting in service listening to a guest artist sing, "I Want a Heart That Forgives" (a beautiful song written by Kevin LaVar). As the psalmist sang, the Lord showed me places in my soul that were full of anger, hatred, pride, and unforgiveness. At first it shocked me. I had just completed a three-day fast where I'd spent those days ministering before the Lord in prayer and reading the Word. I thought I was good, but the Holy Spirit had just revealed otherwise.

Quietly, I asked the Lord to show me what He meant. He answered by showing me people in my life whom I was still holding grudges against. I saw negative events I had experienced, events that I was still hurt and angry over.

The Holy Spirit then revealed the people I felt had caused them; people whom I felt still owed me an apology; and since I had not received payment, I had felt entitled to carry the pain and bitterness that it caused around like a badge; with my bitter heart screaming, "Pay me what you owe!"

I knew the Holy Spirit was right and I couldn't deny it. Not only was I angry, but my anger had turned into hatred which I was masking with self-righteous pride. I then heard the Lord say, "Let the tears flow" as one of the mothers standing next to me handed me some tissue.

Now, I want you to understand that I don't cry easily, and especially not in public! Still, the Lord was telling me to let the tears flow. It was as if He were showing me how to release this pain through my tears. I needed to grieve so I could get over it. So I did. I gave into the emotions and allowed myself to cry. At first I was just a little misty, but then it was like someone turned the waterworks on and I could not stop crying.

The song had cut me to my heart. Here I was, Ms. Titleholder and all, sitting on the second row in church full of bitterness and pride. The truth was, I did feel rejected and betrayed. I was not just angry, I was raging and inwardly I was screaming about the unfairness of it all! Hurt had turned into hatred, and there was no denying it. The longer I cried, the more I began to see all the pain I had been carrying around for years was nothing more than a cry for love and acceptance. I wanted to be loved and accepted by people who did not even hear me crying (and even if they did, they had decided that they were not going to pay me). I desperately needed to let them off my "payment" hook!

In His mercy, the Holy Spirit opened my eyes to see things from His perspective. He also wanted to be loved and obeyed, yet Adam and Eve had rejected him. Jesus "came to His own" and they refused to receive Him. The Holy Spirit departed from Samson (after Samson violated his covenant and cut his hair) and Samson didn't even know the Holy Spirit was gone! Jesus wept over Jerusalem, a city that He longed to gather into His arms, even as a mother hen gathers her chicks under her wings, but they refused to come. Yet, in spite of all this rejection, in the last few minutes of His life, the Bible records that Jesus prayed for the very ones who had placed Him on the cross. While he had nothing but good intentions they perceived them as bad and killed Him. Yet, with no trace of bitterness, anger or resentment He chose to say, "'Father forgive them for they know not what they do.'" Even though I'd heard all of this before, today I realized that I needed to do the same. I needed to cut the cord and forgive. I needed to face the fact that I was still hurting and the only way out was to forgive. So, I began to pray:

*"Lord, I choose to release this debt. No one owes me anything. Rather, I owe you. Father, please create in me a clean heart and renew a right spirit in me. Father, please give me a heart that forgives."*

With that prayer I could feel the roots of bitterness begin to loosen from the water from my tears. As I acknowledged hurt, anger, pain, and fear, I began to see the manifestation of the word the Lord spoke to me months ago: My love is strong enough to uproot anything that has been planted in your life.

## CONFESSION TIME

Okay, so what do you do when you find out the person you need to ask for forgiveness is the person Jesus has sent to help you, lead you, comfort and encourage you, follow, and obey? This revelation came to me as I was sitting in the church listening to my pastor expound on the scripture in James 5:16 that talks about "confessing you faults" one to another and "praying one for another" that you may be healed.

As the message was being preached, I discovered that I had found a seat again on my self-righteous perch and I was passing judgment with thoughts like, "That's right, pastor. You tell them. That's the problem with Christians these days. No one wants to confess their sins," when the Holy Ghost knocked me off my little self-righteous perch and told me I was the one who needed to confess to Him!

*"What? I don't understand Lord? What do you mean I need to confess to you?"* At that moment, I opened my heart to hear what the Holy Ghost was really saying to me, and this is what I heard:

*"Every time you have chosen to disobey me and go your own way, to walk away from a direct commandment that I have given to you and walk in the counsel of your own heart; you have grieved me. Yet, I am the one who has been sent to show you the way. I know the best path for you, because I know the plan. Nevertheless, you have repeatedly chosen to ignore my direction and do you own thing, go your own way, and walk in the commands of your own*

*heart; as I stood in the wings unable to lead you, because you have refused to listen. Yes, you need to confess your sins to me."*

Bam! I felt like a ton of bricks had been placed on my heart and it was getting hard to breathe. All I wanted to do was fall on my face and cry, because I really saw the truth. I realized that each time I chose to go my own way, and disregard the counsel of the Holy Ghost, I had grieved Him. At first, I didn't know what to do but then the words of David, when he had committed that awful sin with Bathsheba, came to my mind:

*Have mercy on me, O God, according to your unfailing love; according to your great compassion blot out my transgressions. Wash away all my iniquity and cleanse me from my sin. For I know my transgressions, and my sin is always before me.*

Psalm 51:1–3 (NIV)

And just like the wonderful counselor He is, He forgave me and restored me! I love you Father, I don't want to ever offend you. Please help me to follow your leading always. I want to be the obedient vessel you are calling me to be.

## LIFE OR LIES

It was time for the rubber to meet the road. I had done enough reading and meditating to see that I had chosen to be deceived by the lies of the enemy, and the only road to freedom was to identify the lies and replace them with the truth. That is, it made no sense to ask God to "let thy kingdom come" in prayer if every time He tried to "lead me in the paths of righteousness," I wouldn't follow. I realized that His will could not be done if my will remained un-surrendered; yet it was my will that was killing me both emotionally and physically.

For example, I knew if I wanted to be successful at losing weight and keeping it off, I was going to have to change the way I think. In all fairness, the Holy Spirit had repeatedly tried to help me, but I had been stubborn and unwilling to bend.

You see, before I became addicted to fast foods, the Holy Spirit spoke to me to stop going to the drive-thru, but I didn't listen and became a fast food junkie. After that, He told me to start walking everyday but I never seemed to be able to find the time. Then He told me to keep a journal of what I was eating, but I didn't want to write it all down because that would take too much time. He later sent me journals and encouraged me to write down what I was feeling—what was eating away at me—but I didn't want to feel the pain and deal with my emotional issues.

Over the years the Lord has sent wonderful people whom I knew loved and cared for me. They would gently express concern about my weight gain and my busy schedule; how it would, ultimately, negatively affect my health if I didn't slow down and start making some healthy choices. But I was always too busy to hear them. I had people to see and places to go and always another project I just "had" to do.

Lastly, the Holy Spirit sent me two professional trainers, a paid membership at my local gym for one whole year, an awesome eating program to show me which foods I needed to eat for my body type (with instructions on how to prepare them and the correct amount to eat) all of which would have worked if I had stuck with any one of them, but I never hung in there long enough to see any significant results.

If I truly wanted to be free I was going to have to humble myself and allow the love of God to heal me and make me into the person He created me to be. Sighing deeply, I began to cry out to God and pray: "Lord Jesus, please forgive me and be my Lord completely. I know now that every word you say is true and is to be believed and obeyed. Father, please forgive me for placing more faith in my way of doing things than trusting and obeying you!"

# A NEW BEGINNING

*"He is a shield to those who walk uprightly and in integrity, that He may guard the paths of justice; Yes, He preserves the way of His saints".*

Prov. 2:8

By now, it had finally sunk in that my mouth was killing me. I had tried to hide behind food, and as a result I was drowning inside. My mouth was the reason for my current state; and it wasn't solely due to what I was eating, but from what was eating me! Word curses, lies I had received and believed in my soul, and words spoken in anger, neglect, and abuse had damaged my self-esteem and caused me to believe that I wasn't worth loving or worthy of respect.

The words I had heard, digested, and believed—negative words, belittling words, untruths spoken in hurt or anger—had taken root and were destroying my life and controlling my behavior. I was now drowning in self-hatred and unforgiveness because I had not taken charge of my soul and refuted Satan's lies and replaced them with truth. I had desired to change but had been too afraid to come out from behind my walls. Humbly, I asked the Lord, *"What should I do now?"*

I felt led to study the book of John to gain a better understanding of how fruit is developed. In John 15, starting at the first verse it reads:

*I am the true vine, and my Father is the gardener. He cuts off every branch in me that bears no fruit, while every branch that does bear fruit he prunes so that it will be even more fruitful. You are already clean because of the word I have spoken to you. Remain in me, as I also remain in you. No branch can bear fruit by itself; it must remain in the vine. Neither can you bear fruit unless you remain in me. I am the vine; you are the branches. If you remain in me and I in you, you will bear much fruit; apart from me you can do nothing. If you do not remain in me, you are like a branch that is thrown away and withers; such branches are picked up, thrown into the fire and burned. If you remain in me and my words remain in you, ask whatever you wish, and it will be done for you.*

John 15:1–7 (NIV)

What could cause a branch to stop bearing fruit, I wondered. I mean, why would the sap that feeds one branch, causing it to grow and bear fruit, not feed another? The more I thought about it, the more I realized there must be some type of blockage that would prevent the nutrients that are found in the sap from coming through. Then God opened my eyes to another truth.

The areas where I had chosen to obey and put into practice the Word of God, I had produced much fruit. Yet, in other areas, where I had chosen to reject the truth, my disobedience had caused a blockage of the Word of God from flowing through, and consequently in these areas, I had produced no fruit. Then when things didn't turn out the way they should, instead of repenting and surrendering these areas to Christ, I had chosen to reach for other things, like food, to satisfy and fulfill my unmet needs.

The truth was, I didn't need to make an unholy alliance with food, or any other unhealthy addiction for that matter! All I needed to do was trust and obey the Word of God. Then, by surrendering and submitting to His will, like a gardener, He would begin the process of cutting away those dead branches in my life and cause new fruit to grow in its place.

I was so happy with this newfound truth that I wanted to scream: "*Devil, the fight is on. I am so tired of being deceived, tricked, and manipulated by you! Your way never works. It never has and it never will.*"

## I'M READY NOW

*"And they overcame him by the blood of the Lamb, and by the word of their testimony; and they loved not their lives unto the death".*

Rev. 12:11

For one year, I have been in a serious battle, reprogramming my mind with the Word of God. So now when the enemy comes against me, I have an arsenal of scriptures I have committed to memory from the Word of God. I am prepared, armed, and dangerous. I am full of the Word of God, and I am willing to follow the leading of the Holy Ghost. As such, it was high time to put what I had been reading, studying, and learning to the test. Hence, time to begin another twenty-one-day fast. Let the fast begin…

**Day One:** The fast has officially begun. It's funny, because I know that the purpose of this fast is not to lose weight but to break strongholds. Wow! That statement alone speaks volumes to me of how far God has brought me and taught me through my studies! You see, back in the day, I used to dread when they (my church or the Holy Spirit) might call me to a fast. I rarely began a fast with the right motive. I used to use fasting to try to see how much weight I could lose. Inevitably I would always fail, because I was mediating on how hungry I was. But now, my purpose was to please God and obey His voice.

With this new attitude, I was surprised when the Holy Spirit brought back to mind a scene I had witnessed from a movie where a young girl was being fondled by an older man. Her unsuccessful attempts to break free from him only rendered her even more powerless as she depleted her energy. He proceeded to have his way with her. Yet today I realized this scene represented more than a girl being abuse. It represented a man trying to satisfy the lust of his own flesh at her expense. It was about a man who had the physical power to overwhelm his victim, a man caught up in his own desires, lost in his own sexual fantasy, fulfilling the desires of his mind and flesh. Then it hit me.

The abuse I had experienced at an early age, and continued to experience well into my teen years, wasn't even about me. I hadn't done anything to bring this on. In fact, the perpetrator could have chosen anyone, and for all I know, he probably did. For years, people had tried to tell me that it wasn't my fault, but I could never really hear them. I was covered in shame and had a false sense of guilt. I'd spent the majority of my life trying to hide, or apologize for why I was the way I was. I blamed myself for being too gullible, too trusting, and too naïve. It was finally time to let myself off the hook: evil men, caught up in their own lust, entrapped me and took advantage of me sexually. I had believed the lie that it was my fault. Yet today, God was showing me that it really wasn't my fault. At last I am finally beginning to understand that it wasn't my fault.

**Day Two:** In my youth, I believed the lie that if I could add a few extra pounds to my frame it could act as my security blanket, one that I could hide under as long as I wanted, and it would keep me safe. My twelve-year-old rationale was since men had abused me because they found me attractive, I would gain weight and the unwanted attention would go away. But today, as I was reading the Bible, my eyes fell on a promise in Proverbs 2:10–12

*When wisdom entereth into thine heart, and knowledge is pleasant unto thy soul; Discretion shall preserve thee, understanding shall keep thee: To deliver thee from the way of the evil man, from the man that speaketh froward things.*

I couldn't believe my eyes. I don't know how many times I kept reading that verse over and over again. I just could not believe it! All this time I had been self-destructing for no good reason, when all I had to do was trust the Lord and learn His ways. Simply amazing! This truth was so liberating to me that I felt like blinders had fallen from my eyes. I wanted to cry, scream, and dance all at the same time! How could I have been so blind for so many years? How could I not have seen this? I knew the Holy Spirit had been sent to teach me how to live, yet I had not even considered investigating, or surrendering this mindset to Him!

Oh God, please forgive me for being so blinded and deceived by my own ignorance and arrogance. Oh Father, I have been so wrong; so very, very wrong. I have destroyed the temple you gave me by keeping it fat in an attempt to avoid unwanted attention. Oh Lord, how many years have I lost trying to protect myself? Father, please forgive me as I surrender this self-defeating rationale to you. And in return, Lord Jesus, please fill my heart with your skillful and godly wisdom.

**Day Three:** It's day three of the fast and I am seriously missing my caffeine. I had a banana for breakfast, ate an apple for snack and a plate of veggies for lunch (cabbage, string beans, and succotash). Tasty, but I really wanted to eat the cornbread and taste just a little piece of my friend's turkey wings that were covered in gravy. I decided not to yield to temptation. Song of the day: "I need thee Lord, I need thee, every hour I need Thee…"

**Day Five:** It's my birthday and I want to party! My friend made a homemade pound cake with pecans and it looks delicious, but I can't eat it. Ugh! I had to turn down a birthday mingle, and lunch and dinner dates, until after the fast. Yet, when I think about the sacrifice Christ made when He chose to hang on a tree for me so I could be reconnected to the kingdom of God, what's a few meals?

**Day Six:** Decided to stay in today, clean out closets, and get a little more organized. I had the privilege of going to see my favorite preacher last night, and I am definitely inspired. Perhaps God will use me in the same manner one day. Actually, it really doesn't matter whether He does or not. I love Him and I want to please Him. Right now the only thing that matters to me is being in the center of His will.

**Day Seven:** I'm on my way to my third service today, and I am so hungry! I felt led to stop at Subway. When I walked in, I saw the cookies and I could smell the bread. I wanted to eat for real! I wanted to order a sandwich with meat and cheese. Even a tuna sandwich with all the trimmings would work, but I came in for a chopped salad with no meat and that's exactly what I am going to have. It was really hard not to add the ranch dressing and croutons, but I know that I'm not supposed to have any pleasant food, and for me that would be pleasant. So after she tossed my salad with oil and vinegar, I paid for my salad and reluctantly left.

I sat in my car trying to digest this tasteless meal. I would be lying if I said that my taste buds were satisfied with that salad, but later on that night as I attended the evening service, God poured His Spirit out on me and I was filled with joy! Man, I didn't know whether to run, jump, cry, or scream. I felt the love of God being poured out in my soul. I was so happy I had denied my belly. If saying "no" to a sandwich, a few cookies, and potato chips brings the glory of God like this, I will continue to say no to my belly's carnal desires so that I might enjoy fellowship with Him. It is well worth the sacrifice!

**Day Nine:** Still holding on! I learned how to cook a new meal. I call it veggie delight. It has tomatoes, spinach, cabbage, corn, okra, potatoes, bell peppers, onions, celery, garlic, and Italian seasonings all mixed up together. I made a pot of brown rice, and now when I get hungry, I just go get a bowl. It's not so bad. You kind of get used to it after a while.

I love the Holy Spirit, because He knows what is really eating you, and why. Today, I feel led to write about a painful event that took place in my life. I didn't realize that it was still eating at me until He showed me. It started when I was eleven. I had gone to the altar to receive prayer to be filled with the Holy Spirit. Later, the pastor of the church, who noticed that I did not receive this gift, invited me to his office to pray for me personally. Expecting to receive, I excitedly went with him, but what actually occurred was a violation of my personal space. That is, he molested me. I was too ashamed and afraid to tell anyone.

This began a pattern that continued for several years. It was our "little secret." Often, he would pick me up from school and take me to the church, and what would start off as a "counseling session" would usually end with me begging and pleading with him to take his hand out of me. When I finally got enough courage to expose his behavior to one of the members, I was rebuked and told not to talk about the "man of God" but to pray for him instead. And that's what I did.

So imagine my surprise when the Lord brought back a scene from this time. It was after one of our "counseling sessions," after I had gone to the bathroom to wash up and noticed the blood. When I asked the Lord why He brought this back to my mind, He said, "This is the time you lost your trust." In my spirit, I knew He was right. I had been broken. I sat in that stall and just cried. Naively, I had believed that the "man of God" really cared about me and wanted to help, yet he had taken the one thing I had to offer: my trust. As a child, I thought as a child. It never occurred to me that I'd walked into a trap, and his intent was to violate me beneath my dress.

I erroneously believed that if I did what he said, which was to come back and make an appointment with him so we could explore why I wasn't receiving the Holy Ghost, he would show me the way to God. I'd asked my mom for permission to go and I'd excitedly gone to the office that day, expecting to be totally filled with the power of the Holy Ghost. Instead, I'd left feeling devastated and ashamed. Believing that I could not tell anyone, I made the decision never to trust another man.

As a result, I had a problem with male authority figures for years, and I never realized why. I was unaware that I was still carrying around unprocessed pain and roots of bitterness and unforgiveness. I didn't realize that after all these years there was still a frightened little girl inside of me crying in the bathroom.

Lord, please show me how to release this pain and allow your love to come through. I pray for any and all readers who have tried to bury their pain instead of facing their fears. Father, please forgive me for all of the years when I turned away from you instead of turning to you.

**Day Eleven:** Okay, it's time to come clean and confess my faults. I gave in to temptation and satisfied the craving of my flesh. Translation: I broke the fast. I made the wrong decision. I chose not to resist temptation but to submit to temptation instead. It all started when I attempted to justify my behavior by eating a few tablespoons of leftover chicken fettuccini, then tasting a little bit of chicken teriyaki the next day from a take-home container. By not confessing my sin, I opened the door to continue even further in my foolishness. In other words, by the next day I found myself inside a hamburger stand to "order a salad" yet, instead of me telling them to hold the cheese and add some avocado I asked for ranch dressing.

The truth is I wanted the cheese, I wanted the chicken, and I wanted the ranch dressing. Then, instead of leaving, I sat down to eat and secretly envied people who were eating cheeseburgers and fries. Consequently, I did not enjoy my salad. Later that evening, I stopped at Taco Bell and got a bean burrito and finished the night off with two potato chips. I see now why it isn't good to hang around temptation. Before you know it, you will find yourself engaging in the same activity you are trying to avoid!

Father, may you, not food, be the one my heart longs to please. *"When I refused to confess my sin, my body wasted away, and I groaned all day long"* (Ps. 32:3 NLT).

**Day Twelve:** Off to a good start. I have confessed my sin to my prayer partner and have asked God to forgive me. I see that half of the battle is reprogramming my mind with healthy food choices. So I ate a banana for breakfast. Around midmorning I noticed a left over pork chop in the refrigerator. It has been there for a few days now, and I am sure no one is going to eat it. I almost bit into it, but then I decided to throw it away. With my praise music in place, my focus is not on satisfying my taste buds, but on inviting His presence through a life of obedience.

The day went well. I was fine until after the evening service. It was around ten pm on a Friday night, and I wanted something to eat. I'd missed my turn onto the freeway and was taking the surface streets to get back home. I must say, I don't think I ever realized how many fast food places stayed open so late. Unfortunately, I decided to stop at one (first mistake) and order a bag of fries (second mistake). I knew I was wrong when I immediately began to justify my rationale to myself.

My though process went something like this: fries are potatoes and potatoes are considered a vegetable, right? I completely ignore the instruction that my pastor had specifically stated we were not to have any fries. Ignoring the homeless guy at the window asking for some change so he could buy some food, I proceeded to have an in-depth conversation with the server about which fries were the best, the chili cheese fries or the loaded fries with bacon and sour cream.

I decided to pass on the loaded fries and the chili fries and just order a regular bag of fries when the homeless man came up to my window. I gave him a bag of carrots that I had noticed in my car as I took the hot fries and was driving away when I clearly heard the Holy Spirit say, "Give the bag of fries to the homeless man and you eat the carrots."

*What?* I really wanted those fries, but I knew the voice of God, so I reluctantly turned my car around and waved the homeless man over to my car. I then proceeded to give him the bag of fries, which opened the door for me to briefly share the gospel and pray for him before driving away. Still tempted to turn around and order another bag of fries, I decided to eat the banana that was lying on my seat instead. Holy Spirit, thank you for challenging me to do the right thing tonight. I really do want to please you more than satisfy my belly with wrong food choices.

# DEALING WITH THE SPIRIT OF REBELLION

*"Then I acknowledged my sin to you and did not cover up my iniquity. I said, 'I will confess my transgressions to the Lord.' And you forgave the guilt of my sin".*

Ps. 32:5 NIV

My behavior these last few days has really shown me that I have a problem with following instructions. It's as if I just have to rewrite the rules to fit me. My family always did say I like to cheat. However, I have preferred to think of it as simply bending a few rules (or creating new ones when necessary) that will work in my favor and allow me to win! Yet, the Bible clearly states *"rebellion is as the sin of witchcraft"* (1 Sam. 15:23). Wow! This means every time I chose to rebel and ignore your Word, I am operating in the spirit of rebellion, which is the same as operating in the spirit of witchcraft. Man, how sobering is that!

There was a king in the Bible by the name of Saul who also had that same problem. As Israel's first king, I'm sure he wanted to do a good job, and based on his inauguration, he started off on the right track. But when given his first assignment, he failed. The same thing happened with assignment number two. He was supposed to kill all of the Amalekites and spare nothing, yet he chose to keep the best of the sheep and cattle, and even let the king live!

The Lord told his prophet Samuel that he was sorry he'd chosen Saul to be king. Wow! You know it's bad when God himself is sorry that He chose you to carry out an assignment for Him! Samuel was so grieved that he wept all night long for his protégé. Upon meeting Samuel the next day, King Saul was enthralled with joy and proudly proclaimed that he had kept all the commandments of the Lord. But Samuel's reply quickly brought his sin to light when he asked him what then is the sound of the bleating of sheep that I hear? (1 Sam. 15:14).

After reading the scripture I thought about my situation and it could have said something like this: "How can you say you are doing the Daniel's fast when I can still smell French fries coming from your car and I see discarded Taco Bell wrappings all around you?"

One of the worst things to be is to be self-deceived. Yet, what follows next is a great example of self-deception. When Samuel asked him about his behavior, he chose to make an excuse instead of accepting complete responsibility. He chose to blame the people. I had chosen to blame my stomach. Saul had chosen listen to popular opinion. I had chosen to listen to my belly, so I could feel good. As a result of his disobedience, Saul lost his position. God found a man who would keep his commands.

It was God who sent Samuel to tell Saul, "Obedience is better than sacrifice" (1 Sam. 15:22). In other words, God is more pleased when we do what He has instructed (i.e. when we follow the blueprint laid out in the Bible) than when we do what we want. He has given us the Holy Spirit to be our guide. We have no excuse to disobey the book (the Bible).

**Confession Time**: Father, I have spent so much time satisfying my flesh, doing what I wanted to do, when I wanted to do it, simply because I wanted to do it, that I now find it difficult to obey. I see now that I have been operating under a spirit of witchcraft and rebellion. As your obedient daughter, I realize I don't have a right to pick and choose which commands I will obey. In fact, one of the commands you have recorded in your word is to *"Obey them that have the rule over you, and submit yourselves: for they watch for your souls"* (Heb. 13:17). My pastor has called for a twenty-one-day fast which means no meats, no sweets, and certainly no fast foods! Father, please forgive me for coming up with my own rules. There are only seven days left. Please help me to use them wisely as I follow your instructions.

For the next few days, I made up my mind to stop all of this murmuring and complaining and get back on track. After all, Jesus, who is the author and finisher of my faith, endured the cross. He didn't focus on the nails in His hands or His bleeding back. Nor did He meditate on the fact that He was being publicly disgraced and humiliated as He hung on that tree; He instead chose to focus on the joy that was before Him. He considered fulfilling the Father's will to be joy. Just maybe if I use this as a motivator it will take my mind off how hungry I am and stop me from mumbling and grumbling about my limited food selection. The reason I started this fast was to pull down strongholds and loose the bands of wickedness, which according to Isaiah 58, are all the result of fasting.

So I purpose to start each day with the Word and prayer. Hallelujah! I'm finally getting this fasting thing right. It's a good thing I did too, because the lingering smell of breakfast would often attack my senses, but I had the power to go to the kitchen and make a protein drink and prepare a pot of beans for dinner. No matter how much my stomach talked to me,

I learned to talk back with different confessions and set the atmosphere with praise and worship songs.

For lunch, I learned how to make cabbage and stir fry veggies. I found it to be really good. Thank you, Lord, for helping me to change the way I think about food and for helping me learn how to make healthy food choices.

# BREAKING FREE FROM REJECTION

*"And ye shall know the truth and the truth shall make you free".*

John 8:32

Today, when I woke up, I realized I had not read the book the Lord laid upon my heart. The book deals with intimidation. When I picked it up, I flipped through a couple of pages and settled on a chapter that deals with the fear of the Lord. The author took time to explain the difference between the fears of man versus the fear of the Lord. According to the writing of Proverbs, the fear of man brings a snare, but the fear of the Lord will provide you with strong confidence (Prov. 29:25).

The word confidence captured my attention. I had been praying for confidence. I had a few unresolved issues that had not been properly dealt with, and I consequently found myself walking around in guilt and shame. Yet, the Lord was using this book to show me that I needed to forgive myself. What happened in the past was the past, and Christ's blood has set me free too! Today, right now, my mistakes are forgiven. All the things I have ever said and done are forgiven. God is not keeping record, and neither should I. Once I accepted His Son's sacrifice, the blood of Christ, all of my sins were forgiven.

As an example of one who walked in this level of freedom, the Holy Spirit reminded me of His servant Paul. Paul persecuted Christians. He had men, women, and children hauled off to jail. He worked fervently to destroy their lives, yet, after he was converted, God called him to work with the very people he'd hurt and persecuted. How did this great man of faith resolve his dilemma? He applied the grace of God to his life, and later wrote that the things he did to God's people, he did it "out of ignorance and unbelief." He forgave himself, and went on to accomplish a great work for Christ. There would have been no way he could have accomplished what he did if he had not let himself off the hook. And neither will I if I don't let myself off the hook!

I needed to forgive myself. I needed to apply the law of forgiveness, mercy, and grace, not only to those who have hurt me, but to myself. I am not perfect, and I will never be. I have made mistakes and will make many more. Trying to measure up to a man's standard in an attempt to gain approval, then turning around and beating myself up when I fall down is not working for me any longer. I am miserable and I want to be free. Lord Jesus, I believe I finally understand! My way simply does not work but your way does!

**Day Twenty-One:** Today is the last day of the Daniel's Fast. It has been an eye opening experience. I know that it is not over yet. I am going to continue seeking God and eating like this for a while. I have actually discovered how to make a few healthy meals that I really enjoy. Learning how to take control over my taste buds has been a challenge, yet you are showing me how to overcome day by day! And to think that this all began with a desire to allow the Lord to show me what was eating me, then submit to the process of rooting out negative beliefs and behaviors that were destroying my life.

Father, thank you for taking all this time to show me the places in my life where I'd built walls around my heart to cover up rejection and shame. Thank you for showing me the areas where I needed to apply your forgiveness, mercy, and love. Thank you for showing me that the longer I continue doing things my own way, instead of submitting to your will and plan for my life is what has been eating me! Father, this day I recommit my life to you. This day I vow to "present my body as a living sacrifice, holy and acceptable, which is my reasonable service unto you" (Rom. 12:1). I desire to be holy and acceptable in every area of my life (my thought life, my attitudes, and my behavior). I want every part of me to be pleasing to you. When you look upon my life I want you to say, "That's my daughter in whom I am well pleased!"

I know now that I can't do it alone, which is why you sent the precious Holy Spirit to lead and guide me into all truth. Through this journey you have taught me how important it is to trust you and to follow your leading. I can only do this by reading your Word, believing your Word, and obeying your Word. For it is only then that I will be able to "prove what your good, acceptable and perfect will is for my life" (Rom. 12:2).

## EPILOGUE

Over the years, I have discovered that the only thing more tragic than the things that have happened to us is what we have chosen to do with them. The words I had heard, digested, and believed—negative words, belittling words, untruths spoken in hurt or anger—had taken root and were destroying my life and controlling my behavior. As a result, for years I drowned in self-hatred and unforgiveness; yet, until I was ready to face, trace, and replace negative thought patterns to help motivate a different attitude and behavior, nothing changed.

I have come to realize the only way to freedom is to face your fears, feel the pain, and allow the Holy Spirit to walk you through your personal valley of death. It is with joy that I have shared my journey with you. It is my sincere prayer that you will allow the Holy Spirit to share with you the areas where you have developed faulty thought patterns and behaviors that are not in line with God's word and purpose for your life. It is also my prayer that when He does, you will not resist His gentle nudges but submit to His leading.

With the help of the Lord, I am a living witness that you can experience freedom and wholeness. A life without fear, regret, and depression. No matter how hard and painful it may seem, let the Lord walk you through the process. Give Him your wounded heart. I promise you He is the Master Healer who has never lost a battle. He know just where you hurt. Let Him heal your wounded heart.

# AFTERWORD

I hope you have enjoyed reading my story. Some of you may be wondering why I chose to share all of this with you. Primarily, it is for the following three reasons:

- The Spirit of the Lord instructed me to do so. Looking back, I believe one of the reasons may be that He wanted me to paint a picture of what true forgiveness and reconciliation can be. You see, the truth is that all of us thrive on relationships. We were created to interact with each other. No one was designed to live this life alone. Forgiveness opens the door for reconciliation.
- To be a witness. I wanted to reach out to hurting people suffering from the aftermath of sexual trauma. I wanted to tell them that God cares about them. Not only does He care, but He knows how to heal a broken life. My friend, if you are ready to release the hurt, He is ready to show you how to walk through the process. As you become willing and obedient to the Holy Spirit, He will bring restoration, order, and peace to your life.
- To give people hope. I hope after reading my story, you will allow God to bring victory out of your circumstances. I hope you will give him your story and allow him to use it for His glory. *"Now unto Him that is able to do exceeding abundantly above all that we can ask or think according to the power that works in us!"* (Eph. 3:20 NKJV).

Today is your day! Right now, God is ready and willing to help get you back on track. You do not have to live your entire life in the pain of your past. You can move forward into your future. Today, you can start on your journey to wholeness!

As you have read, I was seriously deceived when it came to the area of forgiveness. I thought it was okay to cut off relationships without attempting to resolve them first. I strongly rejected the notion that I needed to work through my past in order to enjoy a healthy future. In the end it cost me dearly, and I almost missed out on the relationship that I longed for the most. Thank God for his grace! Fortunately, you do not have to be like me. You can learn from my mistakes and start on the road to emotional healing today!

I can hear some of you thinking, *How? How can I do this? Where would I begin?* Some of you may even be thinking you have too much baggage to work through and just the thought causes you to feel overwhelmed. For others, the fear of facing your past and feeling all of the hurt, pain, anger, and shame again feels like too much. The temptation to let things be is sounding pretty good right about now.

I can certainly relate to how some of you may feel. I had some of the same fears when I first got started. However, when I asked the Holy Spirit to show me where He wanted me to begin, He told me to start at the beginning, and if I may be so bold, I would like to recommend the same process to you.

*The beginning for most will be the admission that you have a problem too big for you to resolve on your own.* At one point you may have tried, but nothing worked. In the end, the pain keeps resurfacing. For some, the problem may manifest through unhealthy behaviors such as overeating, sexual addictions, spending too much, sleeping too much, or talking too much. For others it may be traits of perfectionism, being an overachiever, or the need to put other people down so you can feel good. These are just a few ways as the list can be endless.

*The second step involves trust.* You must become willing to feel the pain again. Let me explain. In order to be healed, you must be willing to go back to the root of the pain, the place where the hurt initially occurred. I know this may sound difficult to some, yet this is an absolutely necessary step in your journey of wholeness. To be free, you must become willing to process the pain. Then, with God's help, you can make the decision to forgive: to release the offense through forgiveness, and clear the trail so reconciliation can take place.

This concept, which is known as tracing (or recounting) can be done in your private prayer time with the Lord. Ask Him to reveal areas you need to examine or with a trained counselor or even with a support group. They can also help you walk through the pain of your past and help you see areas of incorrect thinking. Remember to be patient with yourself. Its takes time to work through the pain and it takes time to be healed.

*The third step is forgiveness.* You must become willing to release your offender, the one who has hurt you. Now, before you close the book, take a deep breath and make a decision to continuing reading unto the end of the chapter. I have a revelation I believe will help you. To understand it, we have to go back to the beginning. *"In the beginning God created the heaven and the earth"* (Gen. 1:1).

According to the Bible, God created heaven and earth and everything in it. On the sixth day, God created mankind to operate just like Him. He gave mankind authority over all the works of His hand and after placing him (Adam) in the Garden of Eden, he gave him only one commandment: *"You can eat from any tree in the garden, except from the Tree-of-Knowledge-of-Good-and-Evil. Don't eat from it. The moment you eat from that tree, you're dead"* (Gen. 2:15–17 MSG).

Adam has been given authority over the works of God's hands with only one limitation: do not eat from the tree of the knowledge of good and evil. For a while, things ran very smoothly as Adam and Eve (Adam's wife) walked in obedience and as a result enjoyed the benefits of a healthy relationship with the Heavenly Father. Then one day the adversary, known as the Satan the devil, shows up and began to plant seeds of discord and distrust in Eve. The unthinkable happened as mutiny took place. Adam and Eve decided to rebel as they disobeyed God and ate from the forbidden tree. Instantly their spirits became disconnected from God as their eyes become open to their nakedness. To make matters worse, instead of coming clean and confessing their fault, they decided to hide from God, of all people!

> *Then the man and his wife heard the sound of the LORD God as he was walking in the garden in the cool of the day, and they hid from the LORD God among the trees of the garden. But the LORD God called to the man, "Where are you?" He answered, "I heard you in the garden, and I was afraid because I was naked; so I hid." And he said, "Who told you that you were naked? Have you eaten from the tree that I commanded you not to eat from?" The man said, "The woman you put here with me she gave me some fruit from the tree, and I ate it." Then the LORD God said to the woman, "What is this you have done?" The woman said, "The serpent deceived me, and I ate."*

> Genesis 3:8–13

As a result of their disobedience, we are exposed to the mayhem we see today. Based on the review of this story, I would like to make three observations:

- Did God do anything to cause the separation between Himself and man?
- Was His commandment clear and specific?
- Did man choose to violate God's command?

Given the fact that God is not at fault, most of us would understand if God chose never to have anything to do with mankind again. Yet, it is God who takes the first step and reaches out to mankind. God is the one who asks the questions and gives man a chance to confess, and, after hearing about their shortcomings, He is the one who makes the necessary provisions so that fellowship with mankind can be restored!

In other words, the offended party, who in this case just happens to be God, decided to look at the problem, feel the pain, then make a decision to forgive. Kind of sounds like John 3:16 (AMP), doesn't it?

*For God so greatly loved and dearly prized the world that He [even] gave up His only begotten (unique) Son, so that whoever believes in (trusts in, clings to, relies on) Him shall not perish (come to destruction, be lost) but have eternal (everlasting) life.*

Father God, the creator of heaven and earth, loved mankind so much that He became willing to give up His only begotten Son, to pay the penalty for something he did not even do, so we could be restored back to fellowship with Him. Once we acknowledge and confess our faults to Him and ask Him to forgive us for our sins, He does and fellowship is restored.

I bet some of you are wondering why I am taking so much time to explain the plan of salvation. You may even wonder what the plan of salvation has to do with my hurt. How is this going to help me resolve the pain of my past? I am saved. I have already asked Christ to come into my heart and be my Lord and Savior, but I am still hurting. What does all of this have to do with what I am going through right now? I am glad you asked.

You see, once we become followers of Christ, we give Him the reins to our heart, and we allow Him to steer us into the path He would like for us to follow. We become imitators of Him as we seek to obey Him at all costs even as scripture declares:

*For even to this were you called [it is inseparable from your vocation]. For Christ also suffered for you, leaving you [His personal] example, so that you should follow in His footsteps. He was guilty of no sin, neither was deceit (guile) ever found on His lips. When He was reviled and insulted, He did not revile or offer insult in return; [when] He was abused and suffered, He made no threats [of vengeance]; but he trusted [Himself and everything] to Him Who judges fairly.*

1 Peter 2:21–23 (AMP)

*Which brings me to my last and final point: the ultimate aim of forgiveness is reconciliation.* God has set the example through His own dear son and now He expects you to follow His example and do the same.

*Therefore if thou bring thy gift to the altar, and there remember that thy brother hath ought against thee; Leave there thy gift before the altar, and go thy way; First be reconciled to thy brother, and then come and offer thy gift.*

Matt. 5:23–25 KJV

As you begin to search your heart, ask the Lord to show you how to release areas of hurt, anger, rejection, bitterness, and unforgiveness. Ask Him to forgive you for holding on to the pain of your past. Then make a decision to forgive any one that you are holding unforgiveness against. Remember, you have the power to release the debt.

As you make the decision to release people who have hurt you in your past from your heart, God will release His power, His presence, and His peace in a measure you have not experienced yet. He will release to you a future that does not include the fruit of unforgiveness and bitterness but a future filled with His love, joy, and grace to help you continually move past your past!

My friends, if you follow these steps and remain faithful to the covenant commitment you have made with Him (when you asked Him to come into your heart and be the Lord over your life), I assure you, you will emerge on the other side victorious and free!

# APPENDIX
## Discussion Questions

*Forgiveness is so important that God says if we don't forgive others, God will not forgive us. Yet for many of us, it still remains a challenge. Sometimes we really don't understand why we do what we do. Below are a few questions to help you process your actions for your consideration.*

1. Do you find it hard to forgive others?
2. Do you find it hard to forgive yourself?
3. Do you have a tendency to pretend like everything is okay when really it is not?
4. Are you holding on to secret hurts, anger, and unforgiveness against someone who has asked you to forgive them but deep in your heart you really haven't?
5. How do you process your emotions when you have been hurt or have felt rejected?
6. Is there anything you need to confess to the Lord that you haven't? If so, take a moment and to write out your confession before the Lord.
7. Has the Lord asked you to surrender something (a vice or a habit) that you are refusing to let go? Examples may include things like overeating, prescription drugs, or excess amounts of TV, shopping, exercising, or being overly active? If so, why?
8. Is there anyone (including yourself or even God) that you need to forgive? Using the space below, give a brief

description of the offense. Then make a declaration of faith and say, "I let it go. You owe me nothing. I choose life and freedom. Therefore, by faith, I release the offense(s). I choose to forgive!"

## HOW TO DEVELOP YOUR OWN
## SCRIPTURE DATABASE

- Identify the areas you have been struggling in. Examples can include: fear, anxiety, stress, worry, unbelief.
- Next, develop a list of scriptures that contains God's personal promises to you. To locate a few scriptures use the internet (they have free searchable Bible websites such as Bible Gateway) and type in a keyword to search, such as faith, hope, trust, fear. The computer will generate a list of scriptures for you to choose.
- Next, commit these scriptures to memory by writing them down on a three-by-five card or printing them out and placing them in an areas you frequent often or keep them in your wallet, purse, or next to your bed.
- Finally, begin to recite them daily, especially when you feel you emotions beginning to rise or you are experiencing a panic attack. In other words, when the enemy begins to plague your mind with doubts and fears, get your cards and read the scriptures out loud. Remember, "faith comes by hearing and hearing by the Word of God" (Rom. 10:17). Not only that, when you submit to God, you can resist the devil (using the Word of God) and he has to flee! It's like turning on a light switch on in a dark room. The enemy can't continue to overwhelm you when you bring God on the scene with your worship.

## ABOUT THE AUTHOR

Dr. Shari D. Scott is an ordained minister, a published author, an Awaken Life Coach and the founder of Developing Healthy Desires and Behaviors Ministry (DHDB), a counseling ministry devoted to seeing the power of God set people free. With the help of the Holy Ghost, Dr. Scott teaches people how to apply biblical truth to every aspect of their lives.

Fueled by her love for Christ and passion for souls, Dr. Scott desires to expose the lies, tricks, and deception of the enemy, in particular to men and women who are suffering from the aftermath of spiritual, emotional, verbal, and sexual abuse. She has earned doctorate degrees in biblical counseling and psychology.

Dr. Scott operates under the premise that the solutions to life's problems are rooted in discovering the love of Christ, receiving his forgiveness, and obeying His Word. Dr. Scott's ultimate aim is to promote the love of God, to display the character of Jesus Christ, and to enhance personal relationships with God.

CPSIA information can be obtained
at www.ICGtesting.com
Printed in the USA
LVHW040422280721
693851LV00014BA/323

9 781637 692585